BLACK AND WHITE PRINTING

BLACK AND WHITE PRINTING

GEORGE SCHAUB

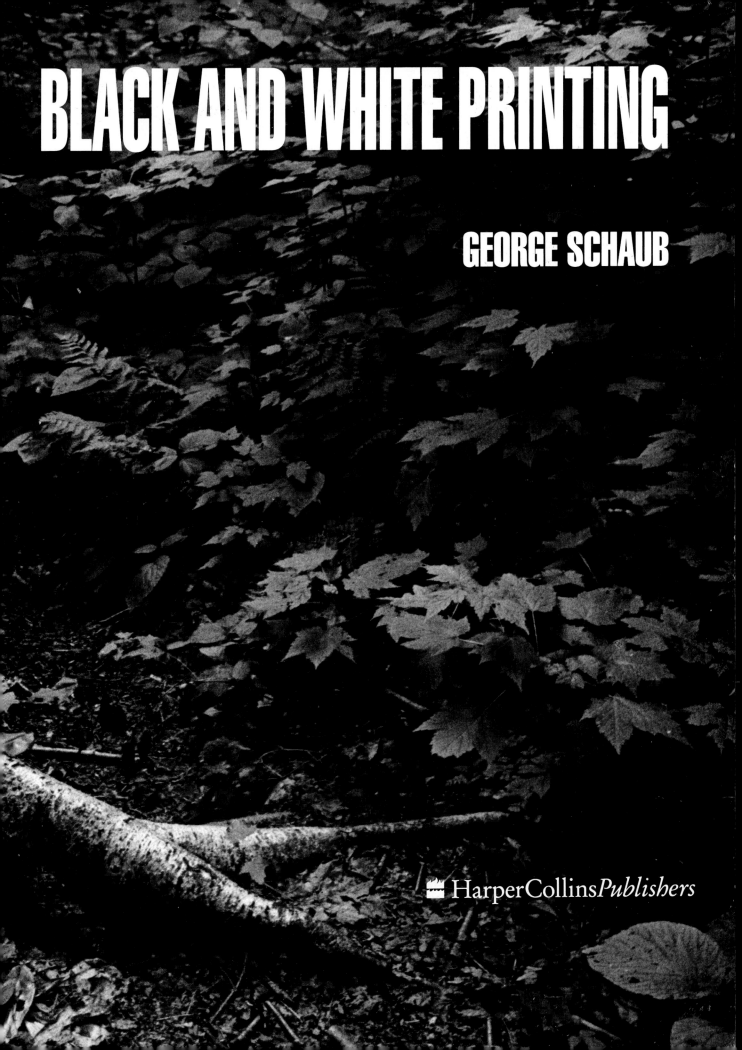

HarperCollinsPublishers

Acknowledgements

I wish to thank the photographers who contributed their work to the gallery in this book. They are the keepers of the light. Special thanks to the manufacturers who contributed their time and energy to this book by supplying photographs, technical diagrams, and information.

George Schaub has been teaching a black-and-white printing course at the New School in New York City for the past six years. He is the editorial director at PTN Publishing Company, publisher of photographic trade magazines, and the author of *Using Your Camera* (Amphoto, 1990), *Shooting for Stock* (Amphoto, 1987), and *Professional Techniques for the Wedding Photographer* (Amphoto, 1985).

First published in 1991
by HarperCollins Publishers
London

Copyright © 1991 by George Schaub
First published 1991 in New York by AMPHOTO,
an imprint of Watson-Guptill Publications.

Editorial Concept by Robin Simmen
Edited by Liz Harvey
Designed by Jay Anning
Graphic Production by Ellen Greene

The CIP catalogue record for this book is available from the British Library.

ISBN 0-00-412636-X

Manufactured in USA

Editorial Concept by Robin Simmen
Edited by Liz Harvey
Designed by Jay Anning
Graphic Production by Ellen Greene

Dedication

To my father, who taught me the craft;
to Dennis Simonetti, who gave me the vision to continue the journey;
to Russell Hart, who keeps me honest;
and to Grace, who keeps the light in my eyes.

CONTENTS

INTRODUCTION

I always feel excited when I enter the amber environment of a darkroom. In one hand, I have the negatives—images made anywhere from a day to 10 years ago. Gathered around me are all of the tools that I need for black-and-white printing: the easel, trays, and miscellaneous mechanical and light-altering devices. In the next few hours, I will bring together all these elements in an effort to create photographic prints that are both a representation and an interpretation of the light, subject matter, and emotions that prompted me to snap the shutter in the first place.

Photographic printing is a craft governed in part by rules. Effective photographic printing combines these rules with an instinct about the way the final print should look and about which paper, developers, and printing techniques will best serve the subject. Each print is an individual matter, dependent on your eye, taste, and even mood at the time you make the print. No single interpretation is better than any other; there is no set way in which a print must be made. Although printing a negative in the same fashion time after time can serve a purpose, it might also impose a mechanical approach on an emotional process. But this does not mean that you should handle certain aspects of this craft in a haphazard rather than a disciplined manner. Ignoring some of the rules of printing can cause some basic but serious problems. It does, however, mean that you should keep discipline in perspective, applying it only when it will have meaningful results. When it comes to making aesthetic choices, your feelings should prevail.

Making effective prints requires more than just desire. It calls for a fundamental understanding of which paper and chemistry to use, how tones translate from the negative to printing paper, how paper contrast affects the final print, and how adding or subtracting light during exposure can cause subtle or major alterations in the final image. Printing your own negatives will make you a better and more complete photographer. Whenever you make a print, you're completing a cycle that began when you first clicked the shutter. You're adding a creative touch that further interprets the moment in a way that no photofinisher can possibly match. This involvement is what makes printing your own work so fascinating; it gives you control over what really makes that image yours. Once you start to print, you'll find it hard to imagine how you could have turned over such an individual matter to someone else. Prints made by lab personnel will seem like mechanical proofs rather than personal statements about yourself and the world around you.

My odyssey with black-and-white printing began when I was young. My father, a printer for major photography studios in New York, had a darkroom at home in which he would work at night and on weekends to earn extra money for his growing family. I can't say exactly when I

For this photograph of a temple in Hong Kong, I used Kodak Tri-X Pan film and a 28mm lens and exposed at *f*/8 for 1/30 sec. Later I decided to use Agfa Portriga Grade #2 paper; I burned in the artificial light sources and the top section of the print to bring in detail. The light spilling across the woman's shoulders enhances the image's mood.

I photographed this scene in Shushan, New York, with a 135mm lens, exposing Kodak Tri-X Pan film for 1/125 sec. at f/11. While printing on Agfa Brovira Grade #2 paper, I burned in the picket fence to render details in the highlights. This image is a good example of an exercise in tonal and textural printing.

saw my first print come up in the developer, but it must have been soon after I could stand. For years, I helped my father "soup" prints and worked in the lab during the summer as his business grew. A few years after college, I joined him on a full-time basis; I then spent more than a decade doing custom black-and-white developing and printing. Eventually, I became involved with showing my own work, writing about photography for various publications, and teaching a Master's class in black-and-white printing at the New School in New York City. Throughout my career, I've dedicated myself to improving my printing and my eye. I've learned that photographic printmakers are a group of craftspeople committed to passing on and sharing what they know.

In keeping with that tradition, I wrote this book to introduce you to the basic rules of black-and-white printing and to encourage you to experiment with some of the creative possibilities they allow. You'll learn which tools you'll need and how to get started. You'll examine why the negative is the foundation of the print. You'll also look at printing papers and see how to use them for corrective and creative purposes. Finally, you'll explore some special effects that you can use for more interpretive printing, as well as alternative approaches that might be right for certain images.

One school of thought maintains that before artists can do abstracts, they must be able to draw the figure. This idea holds true for effective printing as well. Although you might want to experiment right away, it is important for you to know how to make a full-toned, "straight" print from different kinds of negatives. This will enable you to save time and money and to develop a thorough understanding that you can apply to whatever style and approach you eventually decide on. Remember, like any game, photographic printing offers a great variety of play. And it is only through a sense of play that you'll break away from the rules and find your own vision. That is what makes black-and-white printing so rewarding, and is the reason why so many people have begun to rediscover its charms.

PART ONE
SETTING UP A DARKROOM

Why would anyone want to work in a darkroom in these days of one-hour processing? Wouldn't it be easier to just pop the roll of film out of the camera, bring it to the neighborhood lab, and pay a few dollars to see the results? The answers to these questions depend on an individual's feelings about his or her photography as well as that person's desire to become more involved in the craft. Aside from the fun and fascination of darkroom work, the simple fact is that processing and printing your own work are magical acts—ones that have added so much to the photographic involvement of millions of avid shooters.

One of the greatest charms of printing your own pictures is that it is an ongoing process. Black-and-white printmakers still get excited about images they made 20 years ago because each time they print a negative, it is a fresh experience. Each new printing provides you with an opportunity to try another approach, and each darkroom session offers you a chance to increase your understanding of the printing process and to expand your vision.

THE DARKROOM

You might not have wanted to get involved with darkroom work because you think it is difficult to find suitable or adequate space in your home. But if you are truly committed to the idea, you can find a way. All that you really need is a place that you can make light-tight for a few hours and that you can move around in; this space doesn't have to be huge. You can curtain off a small area with dark cloth or partition a basement space to accommodate your needs. Once you expose and process the prints or load the film in a developing tank in the dark, you can carry out the rest of the steps in white light.

If, however, you feel that you can't possibly find enough space in your home, take heart. A little bit of ingenuity—and the cooperation of the people you live with—can do wonders. I once worked in a darkroom that was located in a 6 x 8-foot laundry room attached to the rear of the house. A tabletop was set up along one wall to hold the enlarger; the washer/dryer was against the opposite wall. When printing, I placed a Formica counter over the washer/dryer to hold my chemical trays. I ran hoses from the in/out lines of the laundry service. To get the space light-tight, I glued Velcro strips onto wood and nailed the boards into the molding surrounding the door; whenever I worked in the darkroom, I attached black cloths with matching Velcro strips on the edges to the wood. I put an exhaust fan into the wall over the trays and baffled it to keep the room light-safe. I also screwed safelight bulbs into the fixtures. The electricity was handled by the plugs for the washer/dryer. I was able to set up and break down the whole space in just 15 minutes. And while this darkroom would never have won a design award, it did the trick.

In fact, I have seen darkroom setups in basements, under stairs, and even in walk-in

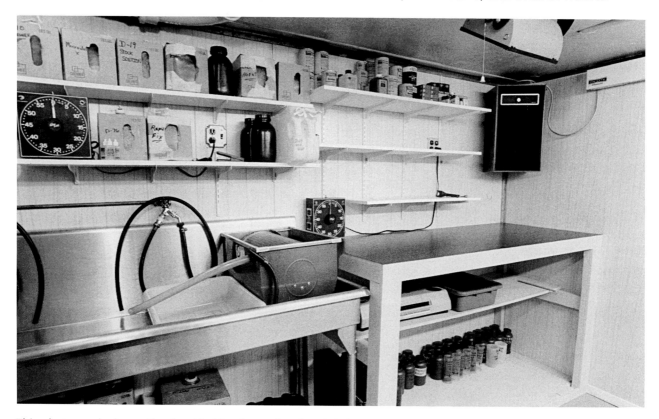

This photograph shows the "wet" side of a well-ordered darkroom. Containers filled with liquid chemicals line the shelves above the sink, while storage containers and extra trays sit below it. The deep sink is used for print processing, and the flat countertop is used for film loading and processing. The Gralab timers, which are needed for film and print processing, have display dials that glow in the dark. This is an almost ideal setup for a home darkroom. (Photo © Steve Rosenbaum)

closets. And more than one traveling photographer has converted a hotel bathroom into a workable darkroom area. Some darkroom enthusiasts band together and share costs and space. Others find schools, photography studios, or camera stores and rent darkroom space on a part-time basis. Once you put your mind to it, you should be able to locate some sort of space in which to work, even if you have to set up and break down your equipment each time you print. (Of course, it is ideal to be able to leave your darkroom equipment in place; this saves time and ensures that your enlarger will remain stable and aligned.)

A darkroom setup can be as elaborate and costly or as simple and spare as your budget and printmaking needs demand. While you can spend quite a bit of money for the state-of-the-art, computerized equipment, a considerably smaller investment can get you started with basic pieces that will last for many years. You can also pick up used equipment from individuals and photo dealers. If, however, you buy a used enlarger and/or lens, make sure that they are up to par. You can also purchase starter kits, many of which are designed for beginners. The same approach can be applied to paper and chemicals. You can start out working with *variable-contrast* (VC), *resin-coated* (RC) papers that are quite convenient in the home darkroom; their plastic base dries flat and fast and eliminates the need for long washing cycles. Later on, you can get involved with fiber-based papers. Chemicals now come in kit form as well, and liquid concentrates have largely replaced powders. These innovations make mixing and storage simple. In fact, the entire field has grown to the point where price, convenience, and ease of use make getting started less complex than ever before.

The fundamental requirements for a darkroom aren't complicated. Also, they don't take up much room, and a lot of the equipment can be set up and broken down with little fuss. A darkroom should: have, or be near, running water and a drain; have electrical outlets and counter space; have some form of ventilation; and be light-tight. All photographic films and papers are white-light sensitive. Stray light causes them to *fog* (darken) or obliterates all the information recorded on them. Keep in mind, though, that other printing papers aren't

This printing area is located in the Parsons/New School photography department in New York City. The enlargers in the foreground are equipped with condenser heads, while the ones in the background have cold-light heads.

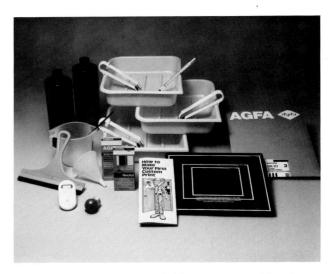

Basic darkroom kits are available at a reasonable price from a number of manufacturers. This selection includes chemical-storage bottles, beakers, funnels, tray tongs, a squeegee, and paper. (Courtesy: Charles Beseler Company)

affected by some wavelengths, so you can use them in certain color lights without the risk of fogging them. Amber is the most common safelight. You can check how light-tight your workspace is by closing the door, turning off all the lights, and sitting in the room a few minutes. As your pupils dilate, you'll begin to see any cracks or pinholes that allow light to enter the darkroom. Plug these up with cloth, black paper, or opaque photographic tape.

If possible, you should also be able to enter and leave the darkroom without letting white light in from the outside. While a light-trap entrance, unfortunately, is often a luxury, it can save you the bother of securing all your paper each time you want to take a break or view prints in white light. Light traps can be double doors, curved or angled passageways painted black, or simply black-cloth curtains. Be sure to use the sitting-in-the-dark test to check for light leaks in the light-trap entrance you set up.

You'll also need running water in or near your darkroom in order to mix chemicals and to wash developed film and prints. Although it is, of course, more convenient when water is available right in the darkroom, I've worked in many spaces with a sink or even a bathtub a few steps away. You'll be using chemicals, so try not to work in any area in which food is prepared or stored. Don't use a kitchen sink if at all possible. You should also have a drain because you'll need to draw off water from washing and to dump solutions after you've finished printing. Washing aids, in which you bathe film and prints prior to the final washing, help cut down on extended wash times. But you'll still need a good water supply to complete the job.

Electricity is necessary for the enlarger, timer, fan, and safelights. The enlarger and timer are connected and require only one outlet; this arrangement helps cut down on the number of outlets. Keep in mind that you'll probably need an additional outlet or two for safelights (see page 17). However, specifically made safelight bulbs can be screwed directly into existing bulb sockets. For safety reasons, make sure that all of the outlets are grounded and are far away from the wet-work area. And, of course, never pile too many plugs onto the same outlet so that you don't overload the circuit.

The next consideration is counter space. This might be at a premium, but you'll need enough room on your enlarger table for your printing tools. Most enlargers come with a baseboard that can accommodate both the easel and the timer; however, some additional space is always needed. Mounting pegboards along the enlarger wall provides an efficient way to hang negative carriers, dodging and burning tools, and even a timer. The tabletop on which you set your enlarger should be level and stable. There is nothing worse than a shaky support that wobbles with the slightest nudge; an enlarger that moves even slightly during exposure will give you blurry prints. Level and secure the table and baseboard with a carpenter's level and shims as needed.

Ventilation is quite important because the fumes from some chemical solutions can be irritating (see page 18). Working in unvented areas is foolish and potentially harmful. If possible, place the venting fan just above the

This darkroom sink, which is set up for black-and-white-print processing, contains three trays, one each for the developer, the stop bath, and the fixer bath. A fourth tray for the initial water bath is partially seen in the foreground. A large tank filled with a washing aid is shown in the upper left of the picture, and a vertical print washer used for the final wash is shown in the upper right.

chemical trays so that the fumes are drawn off from their surface. If not, a ceiling vent or wall air conditioner is better than nothing. You should also make sure that fresh air can enter the darkroom and the fumes aren't being vented to another part of your living space.

It is also helpful to have shelves for storing the chemicals, paper, and other items you will accumulate. The shelves can be mounted under the enlarger counter, over the wet-work area, or on a spare wall. Cabinets are a good idea, too, but might be a luxury. Do everything you can to make your darkroom efficient. You might find yourself spending long periods of time there, so a clean, uncluttered, somewhat spacious work area is essential.

SAFELIGHTS

As mentioned, photographic materials are sensitive to white light, so you must work with paper and undeveloped film under very controlled lighting conditions. When you load film in order to develop it, you must be in total darkness—this means not even a pinhole of light. Black-and-white photographic papers, however, are more forgiving. And while most can be handled in low-level, amber-colored light, some of these papers are more safelight-sensitive than others. In fact, panchromatic paper, which is used for making black-and-white prints from color negatives, is sensitive even in amber light.

If it weren't for safelights, black-and-white darkroom work would be a lot less pleasant. After a few minutes, you adjust to the dim light and can function as if you are in a normally illuminated room. Usually, the lights themselves are household tungsten bulbs of low wattage, mounted within a fixture with an amber-colored filter cover. Safelights come in round, square, and rectangular shapes, and some allow you to change filters for different printing and processing tasks. Specifically, sodium-vapor safelights offer brighter illumination. The narrow spectrum of these lamps exactly matches paper's blind spot—the color light to which photographic paper is insensitive—so they can be quite bright.

Although this illumination is "safe," it still adversely affects the paper when the lights are kept too close to the paper or when the paper is exposed to them for long periods of time. To test the safety of a safelight, turn it on and leave an unexposed piece of printing paper with a large coin on top at your printing station or next to the spot where you intend to set up your trays. After a few minutes, run the paper through your developing cycle. If the area on which the coin sat is visibly whiter than the rest of the paper, you have to either move the safelight farther away from the work area or reduce the wattage of the bulb it contains. This fogging problem can hurt the quality of your printing. Fogging can also occur if the filter in the safelight is cracked or faded.

PROTECTING YOURSELF

Cleanliness in the darkroom is critical for your health. I am not a physician or a nutritionist, but I've taken the time to discover how to protect myself in the darkroom and cleanse my body of any chemical I might have been exposed to. I suggest that you do the same. Like all chemicals, those used in photography should be treated with respect and handled with extreme care. Even though precautions are printed on labels and instruction sheets, too many darkroom workers either ignore these warnings or proceed haphazardly. Since most photographic chemicals pose no threat when they're used properly at home, disregarding the manufacturers' guidelines is foolish.

Chemicals can enter the body three ways: skin contact, inhalation of fumes and dust, and ingestion. Although the skin is a protective layer that usually keeps foreign elements from entering the body, it can also act like a sponge, absorbing liquids and powders. Some people seem to have "thick skins," while others have allergic reactions to almost anything. However, everyone will have a toxic reaction if exposed to chemicals long enough.

One fairly common trigger of allergic reactions is Metol, a developing agent in some black-and-white developers. Varying degrees of exposure to Metol can result in contact dermatitis, a rashlike condition that causes itching and scaling. A very small number of people experience symptoms when they are merely in the same room with this chemical. One solution to this problem is to use a phenidone-based developer that is nonallergenic; these are found in many Ilford products. Another method is to keep chemicals out of

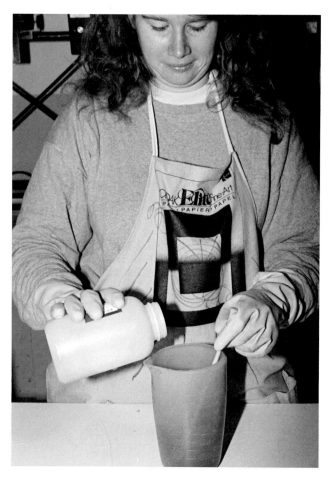

When mixing chemicals, you should guard against spills and splashes. Wearing a pair of gloves and a darkroom apron protects both your hands and clothes. Using a stirring paddle, as shown here, helps dissolve chemicals in powder form more easily.

contact with your skin by wearing gloves. But many darkroom workers object to gloves because they find them awkward. Although I recommend heavy gloves for mixing chemicals, disposable gloves—the kind that doctors use and that are available in medical-supply stores—enable you to have all the dexterity of an ungloved hand. (When you put prints through, you should always use tongs. More expensive grips print well and make transferring prints from tray to tray easy.)

Chemical splashes resulting from tray rocking or inadvertent spills can get on and soak through your clothing and even soft shoes. A protective apron and hard-topped shoes guard against this. Never work barefoot in a darkroom. Also, fine sprays of chemicals can result when you move prints from tray to tray. So be sure to protect your eyes with either goggles or, if you don't ordinarily wear glasses, eyeglass frames fitted with clear glass. If any chemical gets in your eyes, immediately flush them with water for at least five minutes and then call a physician. Follow the instructions on each chemical pack for additional first-aid information.

Keep in mind that airborne fumes can be as potentially dangerous as the chemicals themselves. While your nose will guide you in many instances, you should also pay attention to subtle fumes that can be harmful. The best preventative measure, however, is a good ventilation system that pulls the fumes right from the trays. You don't want a vent that draws the fumes past your face—this only aggravates the situation. Finally, be sure that the fumes blow outside, not just to another part of your home. Printers are not necessarily cranky by nature, but the effects of the fumes might make them irritable. Pay attention to your moods and feelings after an extended darkroom session. If you are drained or cranky, you might need a better venting system.

Because airborne particles can contaminate food and beverages, you shouldn't eat or drink in the darkroom. Never use food-storage containers for chemicals, either. And always keep chemicals out of the reach of children. Whenever you finish working, check the entire darkroom area, wash the countertops, and carefully clean out the trays and the chemical containers. As you do this, watch for precipitates that might have formed. After every printing session, change your clothes and shoes. You don't want to track chemicals into your living area. Finally, follow a nutrition-and-exercise program if you do a great deal of darkroom work. A workout that makes you perspire heavily purges your body of toxins. Discuss your chemical exposure with a physician or nutritionist, and find out which foods help to cleanse the system.

If you take the same kind of care of your darkroom and yourself that you do of your prints, you'll be able to enjoy them in good health for a long time to come. With a little thought and protective maintenance, your darkroom will be a nonthreatening environment. Read the warnings on labels, and follow them to the letter. In short, treat chemicals and your own body with respect.

BASIC DARKROOM EQUIPMENT

The following is a rundown of the basic equipment required for processing film and making prints:

❏ Chemical storage jugs

❏ Chemistry

❏ Enlarger, with lens

❏ Enlarging easel

❏ Film-developing tank and reels

❏ Film-hanging clips

❏ Focusing device

❏ Graduates or beakers, for mixing and measuring chemistry

❏ Paper

❏ Print tongs

❏ Print trays

❏ Safelights

❏ Squeegee

❏ Stirring rods, for mixing

❏ Thermometer

❏ Timer

❏ Variable-contrast filter kit

As you get more involved with printing, you might want to consider adding the following pieces of equipment:

❏ Contact printer

❏ Diffusion filters

❏ Dodging and burning tools

❏ Drying system

❏ Paper safe

❏ Special chemicals

The printing process requires a number of tools, including an enlarger, negative carriers, lenses, an easel, and a timer. Working with quality tools makes printing an easier task, so pick and choose wisely. Here, I cover the hardware used in printing and explore the types of equipment on the market and how each plays a part in the printing process. The main workhorse, however, is the enlarger.

ENLARGERS

Essentially, an enlarger is a projector that enables you to make prints larger than the original negative. The enlarger lens focuses the image contained in the negative onto the printing paper and helps to control the amount of light reaching the paper. Enlargers come in all shapes and sizes, and have different light sources and negative-size (format) printing capabilities. The light source in an enlarger sits on top of the negative stage, the platform on which the negative carrier is placed. When you turn on the light source, the light passes from the source down through both the negative and the lens onto the paper. The size of the enlargement is determined by the focal length of the lens and the distance from the lens to the paper. You can change this distance by raising and lowering the enlarger head. The negative is held firmly in the negative carrier, which is usually removable. The lens itself contains an internal aperture that can be varied in size with metal blades, just as a camera lens can be. The print exposure time—in effect, the "shutter" speed—is set with the timer; it automatically turns the enlarger lamp on and off.

Enlargers are usually classified by the maximum negative film size they are able to print as well as by the type of light source they utilize. For an enlarger to accept a particular format negative, the circle of light it creates must be greater than the diagonal of the negative. In some enlargers, this circle of projected light has a fixed diameter; other enlargers can be adjusted to suit the negative size. These are commonly called *variable-condenser* enlargers. Some light sources yield such broad coverage that you don't have to make any accommodation for different negative

The basic 35mm enlarger shown on the right sits on a rigid single column. The collar beneath the lens stage is the VC-filter holder. This type of enlarger requires VC filters mounted in frames. The professional-style enlarger shown on the far right has a head for printing negatives up to 8 x 10 inches in size. This kind of enlarger allows for heads to be interchanged to handle various negative sizes and light sources. (Courtesy: Charles Beseler Company)

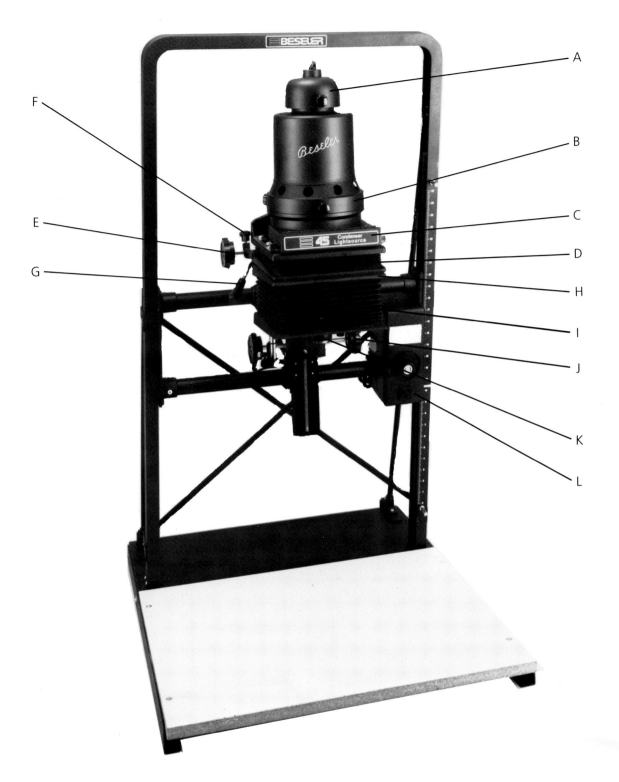

This condenser-head enlarger can accommodate all negative sizes up to 4 x 5 inches and is stable. An incandescent bulb sits within the lamp housing (A) on top of the head. Inside the cone directly beneath the lamp house sits the condenser glass (B). The filter drawer (C) takes 5½ x 5½-inch filters and is where VC filters are placed. The bellows stage (D) beneath it is raised and lowered for different film sizes via the knob (E) seen on the upper left. The small knob (F) locks position. This action increases or decreases the coverage, of the light from the bulb. The handle (G) on the upper left opens and closes the negative stage (H); the metal lips sit between the upper and lower bellows. The lower set of bellows (I) is raised and lowered for focusing via the knobs beneath it (J). One knob controls major focus adjustment; the other is used for fine-tuning. The lens sits in the lens stage (K). The enlarger head is raised and lowered via a motorized lift (L). The easel sits on the baseboard (M). (Courtesy: Charles Beseler Company)

You can make a quick alignment check with a right-angle tool. Here, a thin board is placed in the open negative stage and aligned with the baseboard. (Courtesy: Charles Beseler Company)

sizes. These are usually found on *diffusion* enlargers. In general, the name or model code of the enlarger indicates the maximum negative size that that particular unit can print. For example, a 45, or 4 x 5, enlarger can be used to print negatives up to and including 4 x 5 inches in size; a 67, or 6 x 7, handles negatives 6 x 7cm or smaller in size.

For each negative size an enlarger can accommodate, it requires a negative carrier with a corresponding cutout. The carrier *masks*, or places an opaque border right to the edges of, the image frame. This prevents stray light from passing through to the paper. Purchasing a separate carrier for each specific format is a good idea, although variable/adjusting carriers are available.

ENLARGER CHASSIS

When you first set up your enlarger, take some time to ensure that it is properly aligned. Invariably, enlargers require some adjustment because they usually get jostled quite a bit during shipping or moving. If you have to break down and set up your enlarger every time you want to print, you will have to check its alignment on each occasion. This is less of a concern with smaller models that don't have variable-condenser heads.

Generally, the more sophisticated the enlarger, the more on-chassis controls—such as fine-tuning heads and screws—you have (and need) for making minor adjustments. You will have to use shims to correct larger errors. If the enlarger chassis is severely bent, I strongly suggest that you have it rebuilt or that you get another enlarger. Either option will be less expensive than the time you spend trying to get it right. Remember that an enlarger is basically a projector, so if the negative is not parallel to the easel, the projected image won't be in focus across the entire image plane. This, of course, can be frustrating.

When you're aligning an enlarger, use a small bubble level to check the baseboard, lens, and negative stages. Some enlargers enable you to make minor adjustments with set screws and tuning knobs on the chassis to eliminate a slight tilt. The enlarger's instruction book explains what each knob and screw does. Most enlargers—beyond the most basic types—come with an alignment kit that contains the proper screwdrivers and wrenches for the job. Also, some baseboards have built-in shim screws for altering the height of each edge.

An easy checking system is to place a negative carrier in the enlarger, turn on the focusing light, and measure the length of the edges of the rectangle of light projected. You must make sure that the enlarger is focused so that the edges will be sharp. If the alignment is true, the lengths of the opposing sides (vertical to vertical, horizontal to horizontal) should be equal. Some enlargers also have a variable-tilt or swing control on the bellows or negative stage. Be sure to lock them down tightly once you set them. If your enlarger lacks these fine-tuning controls, do the best you can to make the negative stage, lens stage, and baseboard parallel. With very inexpensive enlargers, you might have to resort to stopping down the lens more than you normally would to increase the depth of field of the projected image. Remember, closing down the aperture decreases the amount of light coming through the lens.

The enlarger column, which is the bar or set of struts bolted to the baseboard, provides vertical stability for the chassis. The column also supports the head assembly and allows you to move it. A shaky enlarger translates into blurry prints. And, since the column is the backbone of the enlarger body, it must have a rigid "posture." Be sure to check the stability of any enlarger you're considering buying. The extent to which you can enlarge your negatives depends in part on how far you can raise the enlarger head. With a given negative size and focal-length lens, the higher the head, the larger the prints you can make.

Be aware, however, that even with the most rigid enlarger, the maximum height is also the most unstable one. Some people design their enlarging table with drop-out shelves so that they can increase the paper-to-lens distance without raising the enlarger head too far. Some enlargers can also be turned horizontally for wall projection, which can yield extreme blowups. Of course, the wall acts like a baseboard and must be parallel to the negative and lens stage. In this case, you must consider paper mounting and lens choices as well. For the most stable system, try to keep the enlarger head lower than its maximum height. Make sure that your work surface is solid, and that slight vibrations won't

rock your setup. If you plan to make big enlargements, be sure to invest in a system with a long supporting column; this is often referred to as an "XL" or "extended" model.

Be sure to treat your enlarger gently. Don't bang the negative carrier in and out of the stage. If you set up the enlarger carefully and avoid moving it around, you'll eliminate many of the causes of misalignment. Also, dust the unit with a lint-free cloth and cover it when you're not using it to keep it clean. As you'll learn on page 28, tiny specks of dust can wreak havoc when you enlarge negatives.

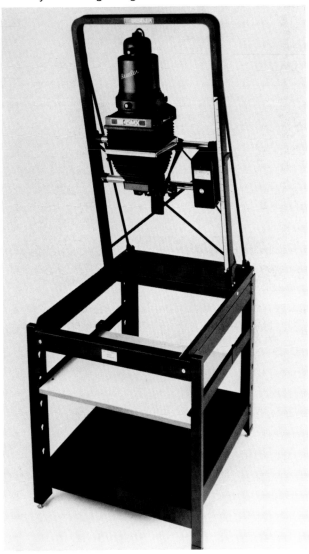

As the distance between the enlarger head and the easel increases, the size of the enlargement increases. However, the height of the enlarger, or the height of the ceiling, might limit the size. Also, the maximum elevation of an enlarger is the most unstable position. One solution is to work with an enlarging table with dropout shelves, as shown here. (Courtesy: Charles Beseler Company)

ENLARGER LENSES

Enlarger lenses differ from camera lenses in that they have a *flat field*. This means that they're designed to produce sharp focus on a flat plane rather than on a curved field, which is what most camera lenses do. Also, these lenses provide maximum sharpness at the close working distances inherent in an enlarger; most camera lenses are made to perform optimally at medium-to-far working distances.

The enlarger lens you choose depends in part upon the size of the negative you're printing. In general, use a focal length that is roughly equivalent to the diagonal measurement of the negative. For example, use a 50mm lens for a 35mm negative, a 75mm lens for a 6 x 6cm negative, and a 135mm lens for a 4 x 5 negative (see the chart on page 25). There are also shorter, wide-angle enlarger lenses available for each format that enable you to increase the projected image made with a normal lens at a given enlarger height by about 30 percent.

Using an incorrect focal-length lens can cause *vignetting*. This is the loss of light transmission at the edge of the projection. For example, if you use a 50mm lens with a 6 x 6cm negative, the lens coverage will be too narrow. As a result, you'll lose some of the image information at the edge of the print, and some light falloff will occur as well. If, on the other hand, you use a 135mm lens with a 35mm negative, the projected image will be extremely small even though full coverage is provided. However, some people "crop" a 6 x 6cm negative by using a 50mm lens to get a greater enlargement size from a particular portion of the negative. And others like to use a longer focal-length lens than suggested—such as an 80mm lens for a 35mm negative—because they feel there will be no light falloff at the edges of their prints. I have never experienced this problem, but some printers like the extra margin of safety this broader light coverage provides. Of course, this limits the practical enlargement size.

Enlarging lenses have adjustable apertures that generally range from f/4 to f/16. Use the maximum aperture—to have as much light as possible—to focus the lens and then close down to the desired aperture when you are about to expose. It is good practice to close a lens down at least two stops to make the print exposure; this increases depth of field and provides a

buffer for any enlarger misalignment or *negative curl* (see page 65). However, there might be times when you'll want to stop down even more, such as when you're printing a "thin" negative on a fast paper, or less, such as when you're printing a dense negative on slow paper (this is covered in detail on page 47).

Enlarger lenses can be either inexpensive or quite expensive. You truly do get what you pay for. In general, lower-priced lenses have three or four elements while better lenses have six or more. Some lenses have an *apochromatic* (APO) designation. This means that they are exceptionally well-corrected for color aberration. Although others maintain that an APO designation indicates a better quality lens overall, I think that it is more important to people who do color printing than to anyone who does strictly black-and-white printing. I recommend splurging a bit when you purchase an enlarger lens, because it will last a lifetime and can always be adapted to whatever enlarger you might buy later on. Even if you have the best, most rigid, and well-aligned enlarger in the world, a cheap lens will give you poor print quality every time.

Enlarging lenses differ from conventional camera lenses in that they are designed to work best at close-focusing distances and have a flat field for focusing on a flat plane. But like conventional lenses, they contain a diaphragm for aperture adjustment. The f-numbers are shown here in the window slit on the lens barrel. (Courtesy: Charles Beseler Company)

Lenses are mounted on the enlarger via a lensboard, which is a piece of either metal or plastic. You insert the board into the bottom of the enlarger's head by pushing it in and up; this places it above a flange inside the opening. Some enlargers have a screw-thread mount directly at the lens stage. When you aren't printing, keep your lens in a case, not on the enlarger. Dirt, dust, and grime can accumulate on its surfaces, thereby causing unsharpness and loss of contrast. And don't wipe the lens with your sleeve or common cleaning solvents; they'll certainly damage the delicate surface of the lens. Use the special photographic-lens cleaning tissue and cleaning solutions on the market. A scratched lens will cause the light to disperse, producing an unsharp, diffuse image. I also recommend that you keep a drying agent, such as silica gel, in your lens case, or that you store the lens in an area of low humidity. I've seen too many lenses with mold and mildew within their elements, especially in lenses stored during the summer when some people do less darkroom work. Give enlarger lenses the same care that you give your best camera lenses, and you won't go wrong.

CORRESPONDING LENSES AND NEGATIVE SIZES

The following indicates standard negative sizes and their corresponding lenses:

Negative size	Normal lens
110	25mm
126	40mm
35mm	50mm
6 x 6cm	75mm
6 x 7cm	100mm
6 x 8cm	100mm
6 x 9cm	135mm
4 x 5 inches	135mm
5 x 7 inches	210mm
8 x 10 inches	350mm

ENLARGER TIMERS

In most darkrooms, enlargers are plugged directly into timers. These are available in digital or analog form. After you set the desired exposure, press the "expose" button on the timer. The enlarger lamp will then stay on until the second hand or digital display on the timer reaches zero. Timers have another control designed to provide *focusing light*. This turns on the enlarger lamp independently of the clock and enables you to size, compose, and focus the image before you make the print. If you have a cold-light enlarger and choose a digital timer, you might need a transformer to eliminate light flicker. Many digital timers can be programmed for a sequence of steps—a capacity that is more helpful for developing film than for printing. These timers can also be set for $1/10$-sec. intervals.

Make sure that the timer you get is *repeatable*; it should be able to revert to the set time after an exposure sequence. This is invaluable for making test prints and maintaining a constant exposure time throughout a printing session. Some printers time their exposures with a metronome and count, while others simply tap their feet. I recommend getting a timer specifically geared to photographic darkrooms. Most of these timers have phosphorescent markings that let you read the dials in dim lighting. Digital timers are usually illuminated with "safe" *light-emitting diodes* (LEDs).

This timer has settings for seconds and tenths of a second, and an X10 switch for setting exposure time longer than 11 seconds. The focusing-light switch keeps the light on. The time switch primes the timer, which passes current to the light head for the set exposure time when you push the print button. (Courtesy: Charles Beseler Company)

LIGHT SOURCES

The two main light-source systems used in home-darkroom enlargers are called *condenser* and *diffusion*. Other lighting systems include a *point-source* system, which is rarely used by printers, and a *mixing-box* system, which is a variation on the diffusion type. This particular system is used mainly for color-negative printing, but it is fine for black-and-white printing as well. Furthermore, some enlargers incorporate a hybrid of these illumination schemes.

Most basic black-and-white enlargers use condenser systems. Light from a single, conventionally shaped incandescent bulb passes through several thick, curved-glass lenses called condensers, which aim the light through the negative to the lens and on to the printing paper. Because of this focused light, prints from condenser enlargers look crisp.

The light in diffusion enlargers passes from the source through a mixing box and/or a sheet of frosted or opal glass, then through the negative stage toward the lens and paper. Unlike condenser systems, which focus the light and pass it straight through the negative (perpendicular to the film surface), diffusion systems scatter the light so that it strikes the negative from many different directions, resulting in a slightly diminished appearance of the image's grain.

Many printers choose a cold-light diffusion head, which is composed of a fluorescent tube

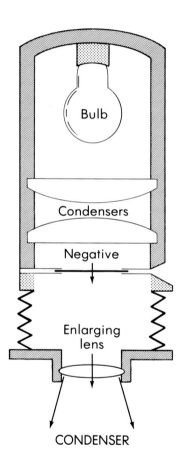

CONDENSER

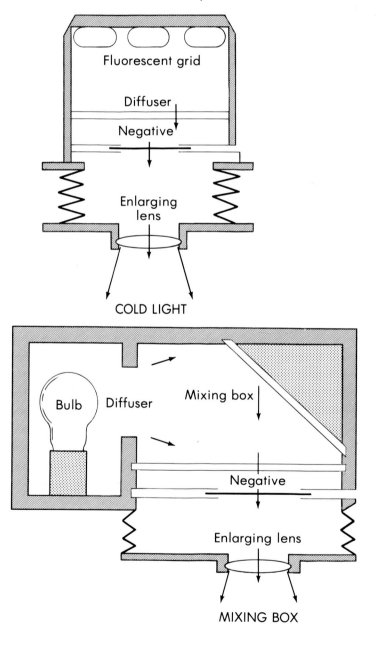

COLD LIGHT

MIXING BOX

These simplified cross-sections of common enlarger illumination systems show the makeups of a condenser head, a cold-light head, and a mixing-box head. Various combinations of these heads are also available.

The negative shown on the right was printed on the same contrast-grade paper to approximately the same print density using a cold-light head, shown above, and a condenser head, shown directly above. Note how the print from the cold-light head is slightly softer in contrast and has slightly less highlight blockage than the print from the condenser head. In addition, the printing time on the cold-light head was about two-thirds as long as that on the condenser head. If you can, try printing with both light sources. Each is more appropriate for certain types of negatives.

snaked around in a metal cylinder, under which sits a circular sheet of frosted glass. Replacing the standard condenser head that might come with your enlarger with the cold-light head is easy; conversion kits are available for almost every enlarger made. Another possible alternative is to buy an enlarger chassis with separate cold-light head.

There are a few drawbacks to a condenser system. One is called the *Callier Effect*, which causes the focused, essentially parallel light rays from the condensers to scatter as they pass through the denser portions of the negative (the highlights), while little or no scattering occurs in the less dense areas (shadows). As a result, the highlight areas receive less exposure than they do when printed with a diffusion system. Essentially, this means that a condenser system produces prints with more inherent contrast.

Another problem associated with condenser systems is that they tend to emphasize any dust on the negative or the condensers themselves. Of course, it is always best to thoroughly clean a negative before printing, but a diffusion system tends to de-emphasize any small specks on the negative because of the way the light passes through it. (Remember, a dust speck might be very small on a negative, but it'll be magnified along with everything else in the image.) Diffusion systems don't eliminate dust; they just make some of it less apparent.

Incandescent bulbs in the condenser system also throw off more heat than fluorescent bulbs in a diffusion system. When temperatures build up in the head, the difference between the top and cooler bottom temperatures of the negative can cause it to "wave." This is commonly known as *negative pop*. This slight waving may actually shift the negative out of focus as you're working, sometimes in the middle of exposure. The loss of focus caused by negative pop is much more apparent in large negatives because of their greater surface area. (See page 79 for solutions to this problem, including a "pre-popping" system.)

Throughout the book, I'll often refer to a condenser or diffusion enlarger and make recommendations according to a specific light source used. Both types of enlargers have their passionate devotees, and each one serves a purpose. You'll notice other differences between the two systems in the sections on paper contrast, variable-contrast printing, tonal range, and print spotting as well.

NEGATIVE CARRIERS

These are designed to hold negatives firmly in place in the enlarger's negative stage. Most carriers are composed of two hinged plates with a cutout the size of the film format (for example, 35mm or 6 x 6cm) in the center of each plate. Some have variable masks that you

Negative carriers are made for each film size and come in glass and glassless varieties. To insert a negative, you open the hinged plates, carefully put the negative emulsion side down within the cutout, and then place the whole package in the negative carrier. The carriers shown in the upper left and right of the picture enable you to transport the filmstrip through the carrier without removing it from the enlarger. Their design prevents you from scratching the film. (Courtesy: Charles Beseler Company)

This variable mask allows a single carrier to be used for negatives up to 6 x 7cm in size. Sliding the tabs on the edges of the unit changes the opening. (Courtesy: Saunders Group)

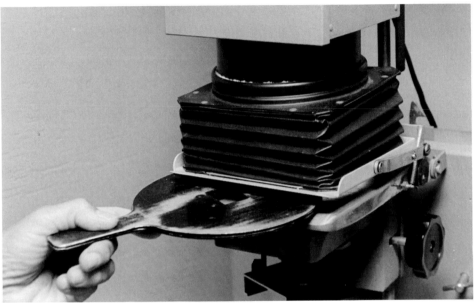

Here, a negative carrier is placed in the negative stage of an enlarger. The stage is raised and lowered via a handle on the side of the enlarger.

can adjust when you switch formats. The inside edges of the cutout in the carrier butt right up to the edges of the image on the film. Some people, however, file the edges so that some of the film's clear base can be exposed with the paper; this trick produces a black line around the image on the paper.

There are two types of negative carrier: glass and glassless. A glass carrier has the advantage of holding the negative absolutely flat between two thin sheets of glass. This design feature comes in handy because negatives—particularly large-format negatives—have a tendency to *flex*, or buckle slightly, under the heat of the condenser's enlarging lamp, thereby causing the negative to move out of the plane of focus. But these carriers have four surfaces that can attract dust and miniscule hairs and can form *Newton Rings*, which are patterns that resemble moire.

Before you buy a glass carrier, keep in mind that you must be meticulously clean throughout the printing session. You must also buy expensive *anti-Newton-Ring* glass for at least the top glass of the carrier.

Although, of course, you still have to work cleanly in the darkroom, you will find that glassless carriers eliminate some of the dust problem. Before you purchase this type of carrier, however, be aware that it simply can't keep a negative as flat as a glass carrier can. Some products on the market try to get around this by holding the negative taut with pressure clips. I suggest using a glassless carrier for 35mm and 6 x 6cm negatives, and a glass type for larger negatives because popping can be a real issue. Of course, some problematic smaller negatives might require a glass carrier to keep them flat during the enlarging process.

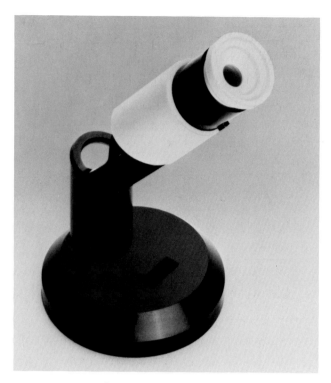

You use a grain focuser to focus on the image grain rather than on the image itself. First, you place the mirror at the base of the unit in the light path and then look at the grain through the eyepiece. (Courtesy: Paterson/Saunders Group)

Contact-printing frames are invaluable for making proof sheets and for special-effects work. These ribbed frames contain slots to hold the negatives in place. Shown here are 35mm and 120 proof-sheet printers. (Courtesy: Paterson/Saunders Group)

FOCUSING AIDS

To get the sharpest prints possible, you'll need a device that magnifies the projected image so that you can focus on the actual negative grain—the salt-and-pepper pattern of the silver crystals that create the image—rather than on the image itself. Focusing by eye is fine, but critical focusing demands a closer view. The best focusing aid you can get is a grain magnifier. These accessories come in various configurations and prices. Once again, don't skimp when purchasing a focusing aid—one should last you a lifetime.

When you use a focusing aid, check the sharpness of the grain at the center of the image and at one-third from the center to its edges. Most sharpness problems usually don't occur in the middle of the print. Although using a grain magnifier calls for some practice, it is the quickest and easiest way to make instant and accurate focusing checks.

CONTACT-PRINTING FRAMES

A simple contact printer consists of a foam-covered platform with a piece of thick glass hinged to it. Some come with a latch that holds the glass firmly in place against the foam. Contact printers are used to make *contact*, or same-size, prints from negatives. In most cases, they'll be used to make *proof sheets*, which are contact prints made from roll film (such as 35mm) that show all the images from one roll on one sheet of paper. Proof sheets are excellent references for filing negatives and for making preliminary decisions about which negatives to print. Many people store their proof sheets along with their negatives in a looseleaf binder. Contact printers also are used to make final prints from large-format negatives, as well as for special-effects work with paper negatives and high-contrast sheet film. In short, this is an invaluable piece of equipment.

PRINTING EASELS

A printing easel holds printing paper firmly in place, provides a flat surface for printing, gives you a place to focus the image, and, with the adjustable-blade type, enables you to change the proportions of the image frame. Bladed easels can accommodate a number of different paper sizes and have adjustable strips of metal or plastic that can be used to alter the size and

A four-bladed adjustable easel enables you to print a variety of paper sizes and to adjust the height-to-width ratio of the image. You can adjust the blades simply by turning the locking knobs and sliding the blades along the tracks. Then you lock the knobs again, so that the framing is firm. (Courtesy: Kostiner Photographic Products, Inc.)

shape of the image area and borders. For example, the full-frame image—the total picture area—of a 35mm negative yields an image area of about 7 x 10 inches. If you make the image larger to fill an 8 x 10 sheet of paper, you'll end up cropping the edges of the image.

With a bladed easel, you adjust the strips to correspond to the full-frame image size, or crop it to whatever shape you desire. This enables you to include all the picture information on a standard paper size with even, white borders.

The surface of the printing easel is basically flat and smooth, except for several slots in which you position the various paper sizes. To load the paper, lift the outer-blade assembly of the easel and slide the paper into the appropriate slot. Usually, the slot closest to you holds 5 x 7 sheets, and the next 8 x 10 sheets, and so forth. Once you've slipped the paper edge into the slot, slide the paper to the left until it stops. This step guarantees that the paper will sit in the easel in the same position each time, so the image will always fall onto the same area of each piece of paper that you load. The easel blades are rigid enough to maintain their proportion from print to print yet allow for easy adjustment via knobs. Although easels for smaller and larger sizes are available, starting with an easel that accepts up to 11 x 14 paper is a good idea. As with most photographic equipment, you get what you pay for. Flimsy printing easels can be frustrating, so make this lifetime investment wisely.

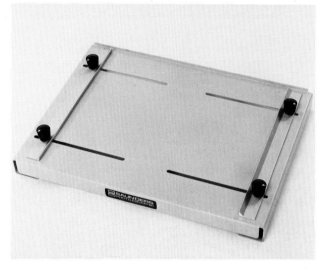

One variation on easel design is the borderless easel. Place the paper on the surface of the easel, bring the edge blades in, and hold the position by locking the knobs. This device permits printing without having white borders around the image and ensures firm positioning of the paper. (Courtesy: Saunders Group)

BURNING AND DODGING TOOLS

Fine-tuning prints requires light manipulation; this is the addition and subtraction of exposure from select portions of the print. Although some of this manipulation can be done with your hands, burning and dodging tools enable you to get into portions of the image, such as the center, without blocking light from areas that need it. Kits on the market offer clever tools, but I've always made my own from thin wire and cardboard or cut holes of various shapes and diameters into boards. (See pages 88–91 for more information about these light-control tools.)

PAPER SAFES

These are light-tight boxes that enable you to turn on white light in the darkroom when there are loose sheets of printing paper stored inside. Many people get along just fine using only the original paper box, black paper, and some care, but a paper safe is preferable. This is an optional piece of equipment that you should consider buying if you often have to go in and out of the darkroom to, for example, check prints or answer telephone calls.

VARIABLE-CONTRAST AND DIFFUSION FILTERS

Contrast is the relationship of dark to light tones in an image. Controlling contrast and making it enhance the image are a large part of what printmaking is all about. Black-and-white photographic papers come in two basic types: *graded*, which means that the paper offers a single contrast grade, and *variable-contrast* (VC), which means that the paper offers a number of different contrast options. A set of variable-contrast printing filters enables you to obtain a wide range of contrast levels from a single VC emulsion. These filters come in sheet or mounted form. The filters are placed within the light path during exposure and produce a different level of contrast depending upon the number of the filter being used, with a low number indicating a low contrast and a high number corresponding to a higher contrast. The filters/VC paper combination is quite versatile and allows you to have a wide contrast selection from one box of paper later (see pages 43–46 for more details).

Diffusion filters are also used in the light path during exposure. They can be used to soften an image to create a nostalgic effect or to dramatically alter the mood of the image. While you can buy diffusion filters, it is also easy to make them yourself. Rub an old ultraviolet (UV) camera filter with petroleum jelly or use almost any translucent material, such as the polyethylene sheet in which you store negatives. In some cases, diffusion filters are used during a portion of the total exposure time; at other times, they are left in the light path for the entire exposure. This is determined by the effect desired and the opacity of the filter itself (see pages 106, 126 for more on these techniques).

OTHER PRINTING TOOLS

Darkrooms tend to be the home for many different photographic devices that were either invented by the printer or bought on impulse in a camera store. As a hobby, printmaking offers gadgets galore, as well as plenty of opportunities for inventors to apply their genius. Aside from the tools I've already discussed, you might want to get a foot switch to operatey our enlarger while keeping both hands free, compressed air and a soft brush to dust off negatives prior to printing, lintless cloth for cleaning the enlarger and tools, a cover for the enlarger to keep dust and grime away, lens-cleaning fluid and paper to take care of the enlarger lens and condensers, and a soft lead pencil to mark exposure data on the back of prints.

PROCESSING TOOLS

An important part of creative control in black-and-white darkroom work is developing your own negatives. Although the primary subject of this book is printing, I can't ignore the critical role the negative plays. All the printing tricks in the world can't compensate for a poorly processed negative; at the very least, lack of proper negative processing makes printing work much more difficult. Developing negatives is fairly simple and straightforward. In total darkness, you wind the roll film onto a reel, load that reel into a light-tight tank, run it through the developing process, and then hang it to dry. The same sequence applies to sheet film, which you can process by placing the film on hangers and developing it in tanks or individually processing the film in trays. (See page 49 for more on the chemistry and actual processing steps.)

FILM REELS AND TANKS

There are two types of developing tanks: *plastic* and *metal*. A developing tank is a light-tight unit that holds the loaded film reel. Its removable lid also has a lip through which chemicals can be poured and removed without breaking the light-tightness. Learning to load the metal reels can take a bit more time, but overall they are more durable than the plastic type. In addition, I find that they are easier to clean and dry. However, plastic reels are extremely easy to load and feature a "walk-on" system; the film is wound onto the reel simply by rotating the side back and forth. Keep in mind that film has to be loaded in complete darkness, so always practice with test rolls and expired film before you start working with important film.

You can purchase various reel-and-tank combinations that permit you to develop one, two, or more rolls of film at one time. The larger-capacity tanks can be true timesavers, especially if you shoot a great deal of film. I suggest getting both single and multi-roll systems because there are times when you won't need the extra capacity.

Film developing requires care and cleanliness, but only a few tools. After you load the film on the reel and then place it in the canister in total darkness, you can perform the remaining steps in room light. (Courtesy: Paterson/Saunders Group)

If you use a tray for the final wash, the tray must be deep enough so that prints can move freely and water can circulate rapidly. A siphon-like setup attached to this plastic, deep-dish tray both adds water to and draws it from the wash.

Print tongs keep your hands out of chemistry when you move prints from tray to tray. The tongs shown here are numbered to match the three steps in print processing: developer, stop bath, and fixer bath. This numbering system helps you keep one tong with each bath and is a precaution against contamination. (Courtesy: Kostiner Photographic Products, Inc.)

THERMOMETERS

A good thermometer is essential for measuring the temperature of chemical solutions. Slight changes in developing temperature can have a profound effect on negatives and can change both the "color" and tone of prints. Temperature changes can also determine whether or not powdered chemicals will dissolve into solution. The best thermometer has a long metal stem with a round dial on top and allows you to take readings in either jugs or film-developing tanks in addition to print-processing trays. Digital thermometers with probes are also available. Be sure to avoid glass-housed or delicate glass designs.

TRAYS

You'll need at least five trays to start with; you can add more as needed later. Trays come in plastic, stainless steel, or baked enamel, and the plastic kind are the least expensive and are perfectly adequate for most purposes. They range in size from 5 x 7 through 20 x 24 inches, in various depths. Always use a tray size that is one size larger than the paper. For example, use an 11 x 14 tray for 8 x 10 paper, and a 16 x 20 tray for 11 x 14 paper.

Trays have either ribbed or flat bottoms. Ribbed trays make it easier to remove prints from the solutions, while flat trays can be used for washing or, when inverted, can be used as a platform for cleaning off the prints with a squeegee or for other chemical treatments.

PRINT TONGS

Print tongs resemble tweezers. They have broad, flattened tips and are used to move prints from one solution to another. Since tongs enable you to keep your hands out of the chemicals, you should always use them. Stainless-steel tongs are durable, but many printers seem content with bamboo tongs covered with rubber tips. Tongs should be color-coded for each tray in order to avoid cross-contamination. The function of tongs is fairly self-evident, but too many people also use them to poke and prod the print to keep it under the surface of the developer. This attempt to soak prints is accomplished more effectively by rocking the tray; this technique eliminates the jabbing that can cause possible damage to the soft paper emulsion and dings in the paper itself.

WASHERS

The final steps of print processing involve washing and require good circulation and constant replacement. Washing schemes range from siphons, which both draw and replenish water in the tray, to tubs, which spin prints and water around in a slowly revolving circle. Some trays have inset hoses for adding water and slit edges for removing it. These trays work fine if there aren't too many prints in the wash at the same time. One of the best washing systems available for the home darkroom is a *vertical washer*, which holds prints in individual slots and removes chemicals efficiently.

This tray washer is being fed by a tap-water hose. The water jets in from the side and provides the necessary turbulence, then exits through a bottom hose. If you tray-wash, avoid washing too many prints at the same time. (Courtesy: Paterson/Saunders Group)

One of the best ways to thoroughly wash prints is to use a vertical washer, which separates each print with a sleeve. As such, water circulates freely over and around the print surface. (Courtesy: Kostiner Photographic Products, Inc.)

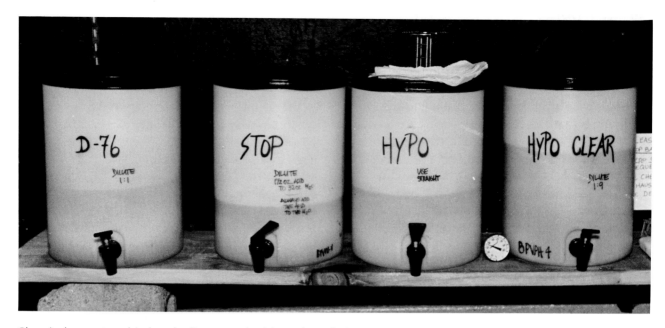

Chemicals are stored in handy dispensers in this student darkroom. Recommended dilution ratios are written right on the containers of these stock solutions. Always mark storage jugs clearly because using the wrong chemical at the wrong time can be disastrous.

CHEMICALS

Fortunately, almost every developer, toner, fixer, and every other chemical on the market comes prepackaged and/or in liquid form. I think that this is better than having to mix darkroom chemicals from scratch, a procedure that many darkroom workers enjoy but whose charm has always escaped me. Although mixing from individual powdered compounds can give you a wider range of developer options, I wouldn't presume to say that I can improve on, for example, Dektol or ID-11 Plus. However, there are some chemicals that you can add to stock developers to change their activity. Some chemicals have longer shelf lives than others, so check the instructions that come with each product. Also, once mixed with water, the shelf life is generally shorter than when the chemical is in concentrate or powder form.

CHEMICAL-MIXING ACCESSORIES

Chemical mixing requires a thermometer, a graduated or calibrated beaker, a balance scale, stirring paddles, storage bottles, and rubber gloves. Although some chemicals come in liquid form, you still must measure out the amount of water for each solution, or the amount of each chemical solution in a two-part, A and B mix. This is where a graduated or calibrated beaker

is needed. Get one inscribed with both ounces and milliliters so that you can work with both scales. Also, if you mix developers from individual components, you'll need a balance scale for measuring the powders.

Stirring paddles come with oversized tips that are useful for crushing crystallized-powder chemicals into smaller bits to dissolve them. There are also motorized stirrers, but these are only for those who mix five gallons or more at a time. Once you mix the chemicals, store them in light-resistant, airtight jugs. Light can reduce a chemical's longevity, but oxidation is a greater threat. If the jug you use isn't airtight, you can create an air seal on it by screwing the cap over a piece of wax paper, and then placing a rubber band around the neck of the jug. Another option is an *accordion jug*, which can be compressed to eliminate the air as the solution is removed, thereby minimizing oxidation. Be careful not to overfill this type of jug.

Finally, always use gloves when mixing chemicals, toning, or doing any chemical aftertreatment with prints. Disposable gloves are the best choice for darkroom work and are available from medical-supply houses. These gloves are thin enough to allow freedom of movement and inexpensive enough to dispose of after each use.

FILM-DRYING ACCESSORIES

Once you've developed the film, you'll need a way to hang and dry it. Most printers get along fine with a thin wire (or rope) strung along the ceiling, clipping the top of the film to the wire with wooden clothespins and weighing the bottom so that the film doesn't curl up when dry. You can also buy metal film clips, but I've always found clothespins to be fine. The most important aspect of drying film is keeping it away from dust and airborne grime. You can get a special film-drying cabinet to facilitate this. Some even come with a heat lamp and blowers to speed the process along. However you do dry the film, keep it as protected as possible during this phase because any dust that settles might become embedded in the film emulsion, and can be very difficult to remove.

PRINT-DRYING ACCESSORIES

Depending upon the type of paper you use, you'll have to find one or another method of drying your prints. Basically, there are two types of paper: *plastic* (also called RC) and *fiber-based*. RC prints can be air-dried without any curling problem, but fiber-based prints will curl to some extent if not dried properly. For fiber-based prints, you can use drying racks, blotter papers and books, or heated metal drums. Drying racks are often made from fiberglass screens stretched over a frame; prints are placed on the mesh screen face down. When stacked with space in between each rack, prints are prevented from curling excessively. Blotter paper is absorbent and literally draws moisture from the prints. Electrical drying machines use a combination of heat and absorbent cloth to dry prints. (See page 118 for information about the various drying techniques.)

OTHER PROCESSING TOOLS

As with the printing (dry) side of the darkroom, numerous gadgets are available for the wet side of the darkroom. Although not having them won't, of course, stop you from processing film and paper, they can be useful in certain instances. You might want to consider the following tools first. A *changing bag*, which is a light-tight sack made out of black cloth and has snug-fitting armholes, enables you to load film into developing reels even in daylight. As such, you can load and process film anywhere and anytime without having to seek out a darkroom to work in; once film is in the tank, all the remaining developing steps can be carried out in white light.

Cotton swabs and sticks have numerous uses in the darkroom, as do sponges and fine brushes. These come in handy for selective applications of chemicals or general cleaning chores. A squeegee is essential for clearing excess water from prints before drying and for certain chemical treatments. Commercial window-washer type squeegees are often used, but a new, high-quality windshield-wiper blade glued to a piece of wood works well, too.

The last item you need to consider is a system of storing negatives after they're processed. I use looseleaf-size negative sleeves, which hold a full roll of film: six frames to a strip for 35mm film, and three to a strip for 120 film. They are also available for larger formats. You can attach your proof sheet directly to these pages as well as add pertinent information to the tops and sides with special pens. Get pliable, polyethylene pages made of archival-quality material (see page 121 for more information about storage and preservation).

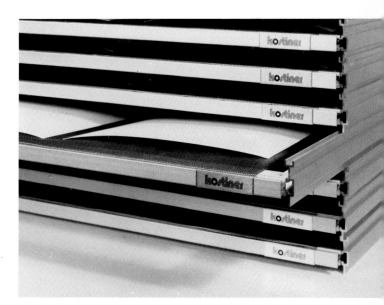

Drying racks are an excellent solution to the problem of FB prints curling as they dry. First, squeegee prints thoroughly, and then place them face down on the racks. Stacking racks keeps curl to a minimum. (Courtesy: Kostiner Photographic Products, Inc.)

PART TWO
PRINTING PAPERS AND CHEMICALS

Photographic printers are inveterate explorers; they continually look into new papers, chemicals, and gadgets. This search stems from both curiosity and a desire to discover alternate ways of working with the basic ingredients in order to find a a new mix. But this search is also a learning process. Each test and new mix brings forth another way of creating an image. Sometimes the changes are radical; at other times, they are so exquisitely subtle that only a trained eye can appreciate the differences— but the differences are there. Part of the fun of this craft is that it is so variable. However, this flexibility can be a source of frustration as well.

As with any craft, knowing your tools leads to more facility, more depth, and best of all, more fun. If you are familiar with them, you'll soon develop an individual style and be able to achieve the kind of images you want without excessive labor or time. But printing tools are more than just hardware. There are papers and chemicals that sometimes act in mysterious ways and involve acids, alkaline baths, and the conversion of invisible images to metallic-silver ones. Once you understand these materials you'll be able to make informed decisions about how they can help you make expressive prints.

PRINTING PAPERS

About 15 years ago, there was grave concern about the direction of black-and-white printing papers. Silver prices had hit an all-time high, and there was much talk about manufacturers reducing the silver content of papers to such a degree that quality would suffer. Many "art" papers of the time, such as Cykora and Indiatone, had vanished, and the early samples of RC papers were not encouraging. Fortunately, all of this has changed. RC papers have come a long way, and a host of premium, or "art," papers are now on the market. Photographic-paper manufacturers have come to recognize the demand for quality emulsions, and each offers a range of materials. You'll find that there is a tremendous choice of quality papers from such well-known manufacturers as Agfa, Ilford, Kodak, Mitsubishi, Oriental, and Zone VI. Lesser-known brands have also flourished, with exotic papers, such as those used for platinum printing, available commercially for the first time in many years.

Each printer eventually finds the one or two papers that will meet his or her requirements. In some cases, the need will be for processing convenience; in others, it will be for a paper that takes toners in a special way. For the most part, you'll be choosing papers on the basis of their color, tonality, and ability to handle individual scenes. Testing is the only way to find which papers are best for you. Happily, there are plenty to choose from, with each type and brand offering special charms.

PAPER CHARACTERISTICS

All papers have an emulsion composed of light-sensitive, silver-halide crystals. When exposed to light and developed, the crystals are converted to metallic silver, the substance that actually forms the image. The primary difference between the two main types of paper—RC and fiber-based (FB)—is in the support material. Fiber-based papers are on a paper support, while RC papers have a plastic, or resin, support. However, RC materials are more convenient. They require shorter washing times and dry without curling. Some RC papers have developer-incorporated emulsions, making them ideal for speedy processing. Fiber-based papers, on the other hand, are generally judged to deliver better images. The gap in quality between the two has decreased during the years, but it is still rare for any "art" printers to use RC papers for anything but proof sheets and reproduction prints (for newspapers and magazines). Another issue of concern among printers is the longevity of a paper stock. When properly processed and stored, fiber-based papers have greater long-term stability than RC papers. If poorly handled, though, no paper will last long (see page 55 for more information).

Speed

Like film, printing papers have a specific *speed*, or sensitivity to light. The speed, or American National Standards Institute (ANSI) numbers, range from 1 to 1000, with the higher numbers indicating a faster printing speed. In general, slow- to medium-speed papers are in the ANSI 25 to 125 range; fast papers are in the ANSI 200 to 500 range. The slower speeds are preferable for home darkroom work because they give you time to do the necessary handwork. Very fast papers are better suited to commercial labs. Also, speeds might vary within a paper brand according to contrast grade; recent advances, however, have eliminated this inconsistency in a number of brands.

Sizes

Papers come in various roll and sheet sizes. (I discuss cut-sheet paper here since roll paper is more suitable for photofinishing labs.) Most printing papers are available in 5 x 7, 8 x 10, 11 x 14, and 16 x 20 sizes; 4 x 5 and 20 x 24 sheets are available in select stocks. The most common sizes you'll probably be working with are 8 x 10 and 11 x 14.

Weights

Various paper-stock weights are also available on the market. Single-weight and lightweight papers come in FB varieties; they're used for both release and trade prints, as well as for the classic 8 x 10 glossy print. Most RC papers fall into the medium-weight category and can withstand a fairly good tossing and turning during processing. Most "art" FB papers are double-weight, although one "premium" or heavyweight stock is also available. The heavier the paper, the more expensive it is.

When printed on a #2 grade paper, as shown above, this image displays a good tonal range and echoes the values that appeared in the original scene. However, the higher-contrast rendition shown directly above, which I printed on a #5 paper, gives the image more punch. In many cases, you should choose a contrast grade based on which one best serves the image rather than on any prescribed notion of matching the contrast grade to the negative.

Contrast

As discussed earlier, contrast is the relationship between the tones—or blacks, whites, and grays—in an image. Perhaps the greatest control offered in black-and-white printing is the ability to alter the contrast of an image through paper-grade selection or the use of VC filters and a VC paper. Contrast control is important for both corrective and creative reasons. On the corrective side, you can, to a certain extent, bring more contrast and detail into prints from an underexposed negative by switching to a higher-contrast paper. Conversely, if certain areas in the negative are very "hot," or overexposed, you might be able to pull detail from them without burning-in by switching to a lower-contrast paper.

On the creative side, contrast control enables you to make many different interpretations of the same scene. Imagine the difference in emotional impact between a soft, low-contrast rendition of a landscape or portrait and a hard-edge image of the same subject. Although heightened contrast tends to a make an image look sharper, it also increases the contrast within the grainy salt-and-pepper pattern, thereby making the image appear grainier. Mastering contrast control helps you go a long way to learning and enjoying this craft.

Graded papers are available in contrast grades #0, #1, #2, #3, #4, and #5. The standard contrast grade is either #2 or #3, depending both on the light source you use and the way you develop negatives; as a result, you'll do

Contrast-grade selection has an important effect on how shadows and highlights are rendered. These prints were made to properly expose shadow areas, with no regard to highlights, in order to illustrate how contrast-grade selection affects shadow-detail rendition in a print. With a #1 paper, shown on the right, shadows are considerably more open and softer than they are on a #5 paper, as seen on the bottom of the opposite page. When exposure is adjusted to balance highlights and shadows, #2 paper, shown below, reveals more open shadows than the print made on #4 paper, as seen on the top of the opposite page. Which contrast grade is "correct?" Whichever one suits your taste and needs.

Grade #1

Grade #2

most of your printing on these papers. #0 paper offers very low contrast, while #5 paper offers very high contrast. The middle numbers, #1 and #4, are also useful for certain negatives and interpretations.

With graded papers, you can usually deviate from the grade slightly by using different developers, developer dilution, and enlarger light sources. This allows you to achieve in-between levels of contrast, such as a #2½. Although standards are maintained as to what makes up a particular contrast number, each manufacturer's grades may vary a bit in the contrast they actually deliver. In addition, papers might vary in contrast from batch to batch and even shift slightly in contrast because of age and storage conditions. This is not as chaotic as it sounds;

just be aware that one paper's #3 grade might be more like another paper's #2½ grade.

A popular alternative to graded papers is VC paper. Here, you have the potential for many different grades—usually from #0 through #5—in one emulsion. VC papers are coated with two different emulsion layers that are sensitive to different colors of light. For example, a blue-sensitive emulsion produces high-contrast results, and a green-sensitive emulsion provides low contrast. Each VC filter's color activates the two layers to varying degrees to create intermediate layers of contrast. You reach these layers and manipulate contrast by using VC filters; these are available in mounts or plain sheets that make them easy to use with any enlarging system. They range from pale yellow

Grade #4

Grade #5

Black-and-white printing papers come in two basic types: graded and variable-contrast. Graded papers are assigned a certain contrast grade, while VC papers enable you to select the contrast through the use of VC filters. In general, you'll be printing normal negatives on a #2 or #3 paper, or with a #2 or #3 filter with VC paper. However, there may be times when all paper grades, #0 through #5, come in handy. Here, the same negative is shown printed on grades #0 through #5. (Courtesy: Agfa)

Grade #0

Grade #1

Grade #2

Grade #3

Grade #4

Grade #5

or orange, both of which yield low contrast with VC papers, to deep magenta, for high-contrast prints. Intermediate contrasts are possible on these papers when you use filters that pass various proportions of colored light.

VC-filter sets allow you to print from low to high contrast in half-grade steps: #0, #½, #1, #1½, #2, #2½, and so on. If you're printing VC paper with a cold-light head, you'll have to keep a color-compensating (CC) 40Y (yellow) filter in place to compensate, because the bluish light from the cold head tends to give elevated contrast on VC paper. If you print without filters using VC papers, you'll get about a #2 grade with a condenser head and about a #3 grade with a cold-light head (without the yellow CC filter), depending on the brand of VC paper you use. You can also utilize a color-printing head with VC papers, and dial in the appropriate filter settings on the dichroic head itself using different combinations of yellow and magenta. Most manufacturers include dichroic filter pack/contrast grade charts with the paper's instruction sheets.

VC papers are certainly convenient because they enable you to buy one box of paper for all of your contrast-control needs. In addition, you can do something with VC papers that you can't with graded; you can obtain two different contrast grades within the same image. (See page 91 for more on *split-filtration printing*.) VC papers have been greatly improved since their introduction in the late 1940s, and now offer very rich blacks and bright whites in both RC and FB varieties. Some printers work only on one or two grades regularly and have found that graded papers are adequate for all of their needs. I recommend keeping a box or two of VC papers available, along with a set of filters, but not to the exclusion of the graded variety.

Surfaces
Printing papers have different surfaces. RC papers are available in three surfaces: glossy, usually designated "F"; matte, designated "N"; or luster FB papers also come in glossy, matte, or luster, as well as semi-matte, weave, and texture surfaces. Some manufacturers have their own names for these different surfaces. RC papers air-dry to these surfaces; the extent of gloss on FB papers depends upon the way that they're dried.

I think that glossy surfaces maximize detail and tonality in any printing paper. RC glossy papers air-dry to a high sheen. With FB prints, you can get a sheen when you dry the prints with the emulsion surface against a heated, highly polished metal plate (called a *ferrotype* plate, thus the "F" designation) and a soft gloss when you dry them by air or against a cloth belt on a heated dryer. I prefer the latter method because the hard shine can create a glare that makes viewing from certain angles difficult.

Matte papers have a flat finish and are excellent choices for handcoloring or other postprinting treatments. However, because these papers don't quite have the reflectivity of glossy stock, they tend to impart less brilliance to an image. Matte papers are suitable for some portraits, landscapes, as well as other subjects. Luster papers usually combine a softer gloss with a slight texture in the paper. Both weave and texture papers are specialized and are used mainly for portraits and when oils or handcoloring pencils will be added to the print.

Color
Although people tend to think of black-and-white printing as being a strictly black, gray, and white affair, printing papers actually vary in color from "warm" brown to "cold" blue. These colors are a product of the paper's emulsion. Warm-tone papers usually have a cream-white paper base, and cold-tone papers have a pure-white or slightly off-white tint. Kodak Ektalure, Oriental Center, and Agfa Portriga and Insignia have warm tones, while Kodak Elite, Oriental Seagull, Ilford Multigrade FB, and Agfa Brovira tend to have cooler tones. These tones can be modified or accentuated somewhat by processing (see pages 52–53).

To fully understand how image tone affects the emotional impact of an image, you should make prints of country scenes, cityscapes, portraits, and still lifes on a variety of papers with warm and cold tones. You'll be startled by the extent that the image color affects the subject matter. The decision to print a certain image on a certain tone paper is subjective and is best made when all the possibilities are known. But limiting yourself to one type of paper is like taking only one type of picture; it eventually cramps your style and your ability to be expressive.

Exposure and Developing Latitude

As you work with various papers, you'll detect a difference in the way they respond to exposure and developing procedures. You regulate print exposure with a combination of the enlarger lens' aperture setting and the amount of exposure time. The duration of the light is set by the timer; this has the same effect as a shutter on a camera. However, most modern enlargers don't work with a shutter mechanism as such; the turning on and off of the enlarger lamp sets the "shutter" speed.

Exposure works in a logical fashion with moderate printing times. For example, an exposure of 10 seconds with an aperture of *f*/8 is more or less equivalent to a setting of *f*/11 at 20 seconds. You might want to use these equivalents when working with dense (over-exposed) or thin (underexposed) negatives. Suppose that you test a dense negative and find that exposure is as long as 60 seconds (at *f*/11). To shorten that time, you can work with an equivalent exposure of *f*/8 for 30 seconds. This follows the same rules of camera exposure, in which aperture and shutter speed can be adjusted in a similar fashion. Like film, many printing papers are subject to a *reciprocity effect*. Here, juggling aperture and shutter speed when working with very long or extremely short exposures might not follow this logical pattern. Check your paper's instruction sheet for the exposure times in which this takes place, and adjust exposures accordingly.

The speed of a paper might vary from contrast grade to contrast grade. For example, some VC papers might require a 10-second exposure on #2 grade and a 15-second exposure to get an equivalent print density through a #4 grade filter. Usually, the speed break occurs at about #3½ or #4 grade, but this can vary from brand to brand. #0 through #3½ grades take the same exposure, while higher grades might require from one to two stops more for an equivalent print density. Many graded papers work the same way, with paper of the same brand and emulsion stock having similar speeds for the lower grades and requiring longer exposures for the higher grades. Keep in mind that this varies from paper to paper, and that some of the newest papers eliminate this bothersome change. Check the instructions packed with the paper.

Papers also vary in exposure latitude; some are more critical than others. In some cases, you can be slightly off on the exposure time and provide extra development to get the density you want; other papers won't be so tolerant. Similarly, some papers can take extended development times—that is, beyond the recommended two minutes—while others don't change over time and will even begin to show a chemical fog if left in the developer too long.

Both the developer you use and the dilution of the solution itself can affect your results. In brief, you can alter contrast slightly by using a stronger or weaker dilution of developer solution, you can change print color slightly by using a hot or cold developer, or you can change the image color noticeably by using a different developer entirely. "Soft" developers enable you to decrease contrast by half a grade or more; these developers can also be used in conjunction with a "normal" developer for a split-development technique that can pull every bit of tonal gradation out of the paper.

PANCHROMATIC PAPER

Because of the limited sensitivity of conventional black-and-white papers, they don't produce very good results when used for printing color negatives; however, there may be times when you'll want a black-and-white print from a color negative. To handle this task, you can use *panchromatic* papers, which render the tones of color subjects more accurately than conventional black-and-white papers. But be aware that these papers are exactly what they say they are; they are sensitive to all wavelengths of light. In other words, you have to expose and process them in darkness. Turn off all safelights when handling this paper, test normally, and check results after the developing cycle is complete.

CHOOSING THE RIGHT PAPER FOR THE JOB

There is no set formula for matching a paper to a particular image. Your choice depends on what you perceive to be the best combination of image and printing-paper characteristics. However, there are some guidelines that can get you started. Then you can discover your own preferences. For commercial work, product shots, and newspaper photographs, either a single-weight FB glossy or medium-weight RC glossy surface is best. These papers are also good for proof sheets and *work prints*, which are the first prints that serve as the catalog of images on your film. Single-weight papers are economical, and RC papers are quite convenient for rapid processing and drying. A glossy surface is the choice for reproduction prints.

Although portraits can be printed on any number of papers, many printers prefer a slightly warm-tone paper because they feel it adds an emotional accessibility to the image. However, more contemporary images might look better on an cold-tone paper. If you're copying old pictures—the kind you find in a family album—a warm-tone paper is more appropriate, especially if you plan to add tone to it or handcolor it later.

Landscapes can also be treated various ways. While a warm-tone paper might be more appropriate for some scenics, take a look at Ansel Adams' images, most of which were done in a cold-tone style. This holds true for still lifes as well. To most viewers' eyes, a cold-tone paper brings a modern, contemporary feel to pictures, while a warm-tone paper provides a softer, perhaps nostalgic point-of-view.

When you get started, you might want to learn about print contrast and how it affects the image by working with VC filters and paper. As you learn more, check out the "art" papers and see how their richness can add a professional touch to your prints. Again, make your own rules, but do so only after some consideration. Don't get stuck on one paper for all your images; there are just too many papers available for you to impose any hard-and-fast rules on yourself. Making work prints of a number of subjects on a variety of papers will prove invaluable. Use these prints as a workbook for future reference.

PRINT PROCESSING STEP-BY-STEP

Processing black-and-white papers is relatively simple. There are three basic steps—the development bath, the stop bath, the fixer bath—followed by washing, wash-aids, and, for certain prints, an additional step that increases the long-term stability of FB papers. Printing paper holds an emulsion that contains light-sensitive, silver-halide crystals. When they're exposed to light, a latent image forms. The first step of the printing process, development, converts this invisible image to a visible one in the form of metallic silver.

To develop a print, immerse the exposed paper in the development bath, and then rock the tray so that the print is fully soaked with solution. Although the image might begin to appear quickly, be sure to wait at least 2 minutes for FB papers and 1 minute for RC papers before removing the print from the tray. Rock the tray from time to time throughout the cycle to keep fresh solution in contact with the print. After the elapsed time, pick up the print by the edge with tongs, and then allow the solution to completely drain off it into the developing bath. Next, bring the print over to the stop bath, making sure that the tongs you used to take it out of the developer don't touch the stop solution. Failure to do this will result in the contamination of the developer bath.

Again, rock the tray so that the stop solution covers the print. Leave FB prints in the solution for about 30 seconds; RC prints usually finish in about 15 seconds. Lift the print out of the solution with another pair of tongs, allow it to drain, and then move it over to the fixing bath. Immerse the print in the fixer solution, and keep it in motion. In a conventional fixing bath, time the print for about 5 minutes for FB papers and about 1 minute for RC papers. In a rapid fix, you can decrease the time to about 3 minutes for FB paper and 30 seconds for RC papers (see page 54 for the differences between conventional and rapid fixers).

You must then wash the print thoroughly to remove the fixer. To conserve water and cut down on the wash time, first give the print a preliminary washing, then immerse it in a wash-aid (which is also known as a *hypo clearing solution*). This can cut down the total wash by as much as 75 percent with FB papers. After this bath, continue to wash and then dry the print. If you're working with FB paper and want to make it more permanent, you then treat it in a *toning bath*. This converts or coats with the metallic silver to create a more stable form. The most common chemical used in this process is a selenium toner, although sepia, brown, or other toners work just as well. (This process is discussed more on page 114.)

The total time for FB prints runs about an hour. Of course, you'll probably be doing more than one print at a time. For RC prints, you can have a finished product in as few as 10 minutes, primarily because these papers are made for rapid turnaround time. Also, using certain fixing baths can cut down the third step by as much as half or more.

PROCESSING STEPS FOR BLACK-AND-WHITE PRINTS

	FB Papers	RC Papers
Develop	1-3 min.	1-2 min.
Stop Bath	30 sec.	10-15 sec.
Fix*	5-10 min.	30 sec.-2 min.
Wash	5 min.	NA
Wash-Aid	5 min.	NA
Wash	20 min.	4 min.
Selenium Toning**	2-3 min.	NA
Wash	15 min.	NA
Dry Down	Depends on system used	

*Fixing time can be shortened with the use of a rapid fixer (see page 54).

**Selenium toner can be added to wash-aid step. This eliminates need for separate toner and final-wash steps.

When print development is complete, lift the print at the edge using print tongs and move it over to the next bath. Always use dedicated tongs, which are separate tongs for each bath, to prevent contamination.

Here, the print sits in the second bath, the short stop. Rock the tray gently to make sure that fresh solution stays in contact with the print.

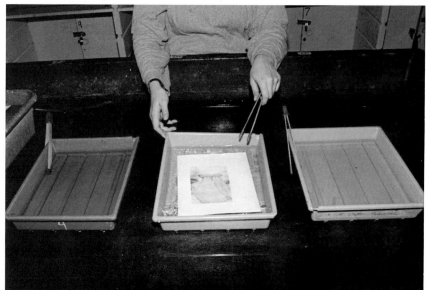

After each bath, lift the print from the tray with tongs and allow the liquid to drain from the paper. This helps keep each bath fresh by eliminating much of the chemical carry-over.

Here, a print is being placed in the fixing bath with tongs, the third processing step. Lay the edge of the print in the bath first, and then slide the print under the surface of the solution via a slight pushing motion with the tongs.

With prints on FB paper, fix for approximately 5 minutes; 2 minutes is the maximum needed for prints on RC paper. When you use a rapid fixer, you can substantially reduce the times.

The first wash after fixing should be energetic, with a rapid stream of water. Don't overload prints in the wash because this will make removing residual chemicals from them more difficult.

PRINT CHEMICALS

There are some basic rules to keep in mind when you work with print developers. Although they are generally more forgiving than film developers in terms of time and temperature (a few degrees off in film developing can have a profound effect on results), you still must work within certain guidelines. Every chemical reaction has an optimum temperature range; for print chemicals, this is between 65° and 75° F. The optimum developing temperature is 68° F. If you work at much colder temperatures than these, the process will be slow at best, and you'll rarely get richness in your prints. Solutions higher than 75° F might damage the delicate print emulsion, particularly if you have a number of prints in the tray at one time.

Also, if your darkroom is colder than the recommended temperatures, you might want to use a *water-jacket* system during winter months, placing your trays inside larger trays or in a sink with warmer water. If your solutions are on the warm side, put a seal-top bag with ice temporarily in the tray; this will bring it down to the right temperature.

Diluting the Developer

If you mix the developer from powder according to packaged instructions, you have what is known as a *stock solution*. You then add a certain amount of water in order to create a *working solution*, the solution that goes into the tray. The amount of dilution from stock is expressed in a ratio, such as 1:2, 1:4, and so forth, with 1:2 meaning one part stock solution of developer to two parts water. If you mix more developer than you'll use in one printing session, you should store the stock solution in a stoppered, opaque bottle. When you're ready to print, you then make a working solution, or dilution. Don't store working solutions because they'll oxidize and lose effectiveness more readily than a stock solution. Most liquid developers are in "stock" concentrates. You just add water according to directions.

You can vary the dilution of the working solution to control both the rate of development and the print contrast. A highly dilute developer works more slowly than a concentrated one. Higher concentrations produce more contrasty results. If you follow the recommendations for dilutions in the manufacturer's spec sheets, you

won't be far off; modify the specs as you deem necessary, but keep in mind that too much dilution makes for a slow and weak developer. In fact, some developers allow you to modify contrast through dilution; however, I find that it is best to make contrast-grade changes via the paper, not the developer.

Developing Time

Developing time varies with the type of paper you use. For RC papers, you should develop between 1 and 2 minutes, even though you might see what looks like a finished print before that time. If an RC print still looks pale after 90 seconds, increasing development won't do anything; you should give the next one more exposure time. This is also true for FB prints, but with these the developing time should be at least 2 minutes. After that length of time, you'll know what you've got, but you can leave the paper in the developer another minute or so to bring it along even further. Changes won't be dramatic after that time, but the little extra developing time might just give the paper the touch it needs, particularly in the *highlight* (near-white) areas. But be careful not to leave a print in too long because it'll fog. Conversely, if the print comes up too quickly in the developer and you see it going too dark, you can't save it by pulling it out of the developer before it is done. This will result in mottled blacks and a weak, muddy appearance in the print.

Developing solutions weaken as you use them. You'll know this has happened when prints develop very slowly or when a thin layer of silt deposit begins to form at the bottom of the tray. The number of prints this takes depends on both the amount of the developer and the dilution and type of print developer you're using.

PRINT COLOR AND PAPER DEVELOPERS

As discussed earlier, printing papers have a certain "color," ranging from cold (or bluish-black with bright whites) to warm (brownish-black with creamy whites). You can neutralize or emphasize this color by using certain print developers. For example, Agfa Portriga, a warm-tone paper, yields a warm black when developed in Kodak Selectol developer and a cooler tone when developed in Kodak Dektol. Ilford Galerie shows a warmer tone when processed in Selectol, and a cool tone when souped in Dektol. There are dozens of papers and paper developers, as well as formulations you can mix yourself, on the market today. The possibilities seem endless, but you'll find just the right combination for each image or group of images through testing and experimentation.

When you have a new batch of paper, run a sheet or two through every new developer you use and create a catalog for future reference. (A "batch of paper" refers to paper in the same emulsion run. While manufacturers do their best to maintain standards in paper made six months apart, there might be some variations in the mix, some of which will affect paper color. Some manufacturers print the emulsion number codes on the paper box. You should always test a new box of paper before making any assumptions about how it will perform.)

If you want to emphasize the warmth of a warm-tone paper, such as Agfa Portriga or Kodak Ektalure, use a warm-tone developer; these include Kodak Selectol or Edwal Platinum II. If colder tones are needed, use a cold-tone paper, such as Agfa Brovira or Oriental Seagull, with Kodak Dektol or Ilford Bromophen. Shifts in color can be dramatic or subtle, depending on the way you combine paper with developer and, with some developers, how warm or cold the solution is and the how diluted the stock mix is. However, some papers resist any color variance; these are commercial papers used in photofinishing labs that must maintain a steady color throughout long print runs.

Matching paper color from printing session to printing session can be a problem because any number of variables come into play. To keep colors within a tight latitude, follow strict processing procedures, and make sure that developer temperature, dilution, and freshness are consistent from session to session. In addition, some papers might vary in color from grade to grade and even from batch to batch. Although strict matching of paper color might not seem important when you make prints one at a time, it can have a profound effect on the look of a portfolio when print matching will usually be discerned by a more trained eye. There are enough variations within the paper/developer combinations to give you a full range of tones, from warm brown through neutral to a bluish-black. Keep notes as you

experiment, and learn the basics of cool/warm effects as you print.

DEVELOPERS AND PRINT COLOR

Although the following list is far from comprehensive, it is a basic guide to how developers can affect print color. If the developer you use doesn't appear here or if you're in doubt about the paper you're using, check the instruction sheet that comes with the materials. Papers will usually say "warm tone," "neutral," or "cold tone" on the packaging. Again, read the instruction sheet to learn how the developer affects print color. The effects of some vary with developer dilution and solution temperature.

Agfa Neutol: A developer that yields cold tones on cold-tone papers, neutral tones on neutral papers, and cooler variations on warm-tone papers.

Edwal LPD: One of the variable-tone developers. Dilute 1:1 for cold-tones, 1:4 for warm tones, and 1:2 for neutral tones on appropriate papers. Follow recommended developing times.

Edwal Platinum II: A liquid-concentrate warm-tone developer for warm or neutral tones on warm-tone paper and neutral tones on neutral- and cold-tone papers.

Ilford Bromophen: A similar formula to Dektol. Substitutes phenidone for metol as one of its developing agents. Metol might cause allergic reactions in some people; Bromophen eliminates this reaction.

Ilford Universal: A liquid concentrate for cold-tone response on cold-tone papers, neutral tones on neutral papers, and cooler variations on warm-tone papers.

Kodak Dektol: A universal paper developer for emphasizing cold-tones on cold-tone papers. Yields neutral tones on neutral papers and a cooler variation on warm-tone papers.

Kodak Selectol: A warm-tone developer used specifically for bringing full warm tones to warm-tone papers.

Kodak Selectol Soft: For most papers, can be used to soften contrast on graded papers by as much as $2/3$ contrast steps.

THE STOP BATH

Not much can be said about the second step in print processing. In fact, some printers eliminate the stop bath and replace it with a water bath. The stop bath is an acidic solution that literally stops print development by neutralizing the alkalinity of the developer remaining in the print. This happens quickly, but most printers make sure that the stop bath has done its job by leaving the print in the bath for as long as 30 seconds. You can dispense with this rather sharp-smelling chemical by using a water bath because the next step, the fixer bath, is also an acidic solution. The water bath slows development via dilution, but doesn't halt it entirely. As a result, for the greatest control you should use stop. Also, the stop bath neutralizes the developer, thereby helping to keep the fixer bath fresh for a longer period of time. This is why I prefer using the stop bath.

The easiest and safest form of stop is Kodak or another manufacturer's "Indicator Stop Bath," a liquid concentrate. Mix according to packaged directions. The "Indicator" in the name means that the bath turns purple when it's exhausted; this is a good visual check when you're running lots of prints during a session.

THE FIXER BATH

As mentioned, the fixer bath performs the all-important function of removing unexposed silver halides. Once the bath does its work, you have to remove the fixer, also called *hypo*, from the paper. But when you fix prints, you must be sure that the bath is fresh. Exhausted fixer simply won't be effective regardless of how long you leave the print in the solution. Even longer washing times after the fix won't compensate for this. Proper fixation requires a fresh bath.

There are two types of fixer on the market. The most common is an acid fixer (in liquid concentrate or powder form) composed of sodium thiosulfate and sodium sulfite. FB prints take about 5 minutes to "clear" in this fixer; RC prints, about 2 minutes. A second type, called *rapid fixer*, is based on the same formula with the addition of ammonium chloride. This chemical does exactly what its name implies: it fixes rapidly, from 30 seconds to 3 minutes, depending on the fixer itself and whether you're working with RC or FB papers. RC papers fix more quickly. While the rapid fixer speeds

production, you must avoid overfixing in it because it will be difficult to remove later.

Fixers might contain a hardening agent for use on delicate emulsions. Hardeners are useful when you want a slick, glass-like sheen on glossy FB papers that are being dried with the ferrotype-plate method. This holds true when you want a similar finish on glossy RC prints. But a hardener can cause problems if you plan to tone a paper after processing because it can make the paper surface resistant to the toning solution. Some liquid fixers have "A" and "B" bottles; the "B" bottle is usually the hardening agent. Powder and liquid fixer come in both hardener-incorporated and hardener-free varieties. Of course, nonhardened paper is a bit more delicate than when no hardener is used, so handle wet and dry prints carefully.

There are a number of ways to maintain the freshness of the fixer. You should use fresh hypo after 30 or so 8 x 10 prints per fresh 11 x 14 tray of solution; this replenishing frequency should protect you against loading up on contaminants. Another option is to use a two-bath setup. Start with two fresh trays of hypo and move prints through both of them, half the total fixing time in the first and the second half in the second. After approximately 30 prints have been run through a fresh, full 11 x 14 tray of fixer, dump the first tray and move the second tray into the first position. Next, mix a fresh bath for the second tray. This system is almost foolproof. You can check the freshness of the hypo bath by using Edwal Hypo-Chek or a similar product. Squirt a bit of the solution into the fixer. If a white precipitate forms, you need a fresh bath.

Once fixing is complete, you must remove as much of the fixer from the print as possible. High levels of fixer left in the emulsion can result in staining and rapid deterioration of the image over time. The best way to remove fix is by thorough washing and treatment in a washing-aid. If you choose not to go with a wash-aid, you'll have to wash FB prints for several hours. RC prints are made for rapid processing, and because of their plastic base absorb less fix than a FB material and don't require a wash-aid. Wash-aid, also known as "Perma-Wash," "Hypo-Clearing Agent," and other names, means less time in the darkroom and a lower water bill.

PROCESSING FOR PERMANENCE

Before the final wash, you might choose to take the processing a step further by treating prints in a toning bath. This protects the image by making the silver a more stable compound. As a result, it is more resistant to fading and staining. The most commonly used toners for this step are sepia, brown, and selenium (see page 114 for more information). You can mix your own toners, but happily most are readily available in kit form. All of the toners mentioned convert or combine with the metallic silver.

The universal standard for conversion is Kodak Rapid Selenium toner, which is available in liquid-concentrate form. When used in fairly concentrated form, it can be used to impart a magenta or slightly reddish-brown color to the print. However, when used in a 1:32 (or slightly higher) dilution, it converts without altering print color. While sepia and brown toners also offer protection, they have a marked effect on print color, turning even cold-tone prints a yellow- to reddish-brown. Toning with sepia, brown, and similar chemistry must be done in separate baths. Rapid Selenium toner, on the other hand, can be added directly to the wash-aid solution step, which eliminates posttreatment time and bother. But realize that toned prints require additional protection to keep them safe from environmental dangers (see page 114).

The tray on the right contains a wash-aid, which helps remove fixer. The wash tray on the left has a siphon attachment that adds fresh water while it draws water away from the tub. After immersion in the wash-aid for about 5 minutes, prints are moved over to the final wash. The rotary washer shown below is another type of final-wash setup. A steady stream of fresh water spins the washer while a drain eliminates contaminated water. It also circulates the prints and does a good job of removing fixer.

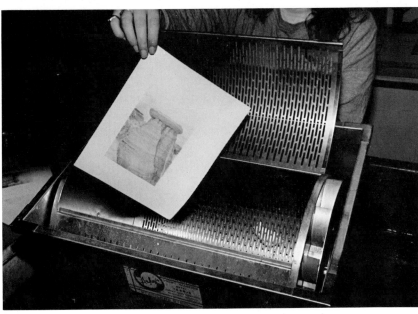

Before you place prints on drying racks, blotters, or any other drying device, be sure to remove excess water from both the front and back of the paper with a squeegee. Use a number of gentle strokes rather than one pull to get all of the water off the paper, as shown on the right. The electrical drum dryer shown below uses heat and absorbent cloth to dry prints. If you want a hard, glossy finish with glossy paper, dry the prints so that they face the metal drum during drying; for a softer sheen, dry the prints so that they face away from the metal. These dryers are often found in schools and wherever volume processing is done.

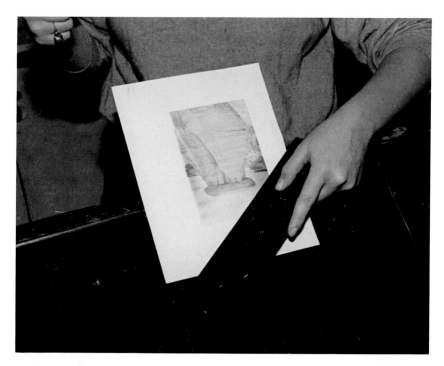

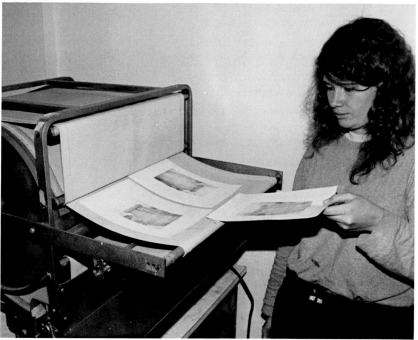

OTHER DARKROOM CHEMICALS

If you ever venture into the darkroom of a veteran printer, you'll probably notice an odd array of bottles filled with strange and mysterious powders. These alchemists often mix their own developers, starting from scratch and adding their own personal touches to their brews. If this is your bent, there are numerous books with formulas for almost every type of darkroom chemistry imaginable, including tried-and-true methods and some that have been left by the wayside. I prefer premixed and premeasured chemistry. I've always found that the wide variety of commercially available chemicals served my needs. However, I do occasionally use some chemicals that add a certain flavor to select images; these include benzotriazole, sodium carbonate, potassium bromide, and potassium ferricyanide.

Benzotriazole, which is available in liquid form, can be used to increase the cold tone of cold-tone papers. Add the developer to taste, experiment with different strengths, and check results. Start with about six drops of benzotriazole to a gallon of solution. Sodium carbonate, which is available in powder form, helps boost the activity of the developer and, as a result, can give you deeper blacks. Make a solution by mixing 2 ounces of sodium carbonate to 1 quart of water, and then add 3 to 6 ounces of this solution to a gallon tray of developer. This can also be used in a pinch to rejuvenate tired developer; this tip comes in handy when your "soup" is almost exhausted and you have only a few more prints to put through for the day.

Potassium bromide is good for reclaiming fogged papers (fogged due to age, not light) and brightening print highlights. Mix a 10 percent solution (1 ounce of potassium bromide to 10 ounces of water), and soak the old, tired paper in it prior to inserting it in your developer. This system seems to help papers hidden on the back of a darkroom shelf for a few years or for use with out-of-date papers that are often sold at enormous discounts in photo stores. Adding the solution straight to the developer boosts print contrast slightly on flat, grayish prints; however, it is not a cure-all for poor contrast-grade selection. Finally, potassium ferricyanide, used as a separate bath after prints are processed, is one of my favorite darkroom helpers. It is useful for rescuing overprinted images and for adding very selective touches in print finishing (see "Bleaching/Reduction" on page 116).

Tray cleaners, sold by many manufacturers, are also very helpful chemicals to keep on hand in the darkroom. After extensive use, the bottom of developing trays can turn a silvery black, a result of by-products of the developing process. Tray cleaner removes this stain and ensures that no smudges will form on prints sitting in the tray. Be careful when using tray cleaner because it is quite caustic. I also keep a supply of a wetting agent on hand. This chemical is essential for film as well as for getting a smooth finish on ferrotyped prints. Soak prints in a very mild solution of wetting agent before heat-drum drying.

You'll soon see that other chemicals, both household and strictly photographic, are useful in the darkroom. Having gathered your tools, you can begin to consider the prints and the negatives. Although negatives aren't the primary subject of this book, they are an essential ingredient in the black-and-white printing process. In fact, they can make subsequent printing either an easy task or one that requires you to always catch up.

PART THREE

THE BLACK-AND-WHITE NEGATIVE

When you make a proper exposure and develop in a way that brings out all of the tones of the original scene, you have a negative that simplifies printing. Failure to follow the rules of developing limits your creative options later. Many books about black-and-white negative control have been written, so I'm just giving an overview of what constitutes a good negative and encouraging you to pursue this subject further on your own.

The black-and-white negative is a reversal of the brightness values in the original scene. When you make a print, you reverse the negative to a positive. The object of correct exposure and development is to obtain a negative that captures as wide a range as possible of those brightness values, which are also referred to as tones. However, this isn't always simple.

Too much light yields an over-exposed negative. This, in turn, can result in unwanted increases in grain and harsh, too-dense highlights. Too little light means that the scene is underexposed, so there might be loss of image information in the darker or shadow areas. When carried to the extreme, under- and overexposure might make certain negatives unprintable or at least cause a serious loss in image quality.

DETERMINING CORRECT EXPOSURE

Correct exposure depends on a number of factors, all of which affect results to certain degrees. These include the speed and character of the film in use, the range of brightnesses in the scene, the brightness values you consider important, and the aperture and/or shutter speed required to capture a specific amount of light. All of these are a function of camera control. After exposure, development of the film also partially determines results. At this point, you must consider the type of developer you intend to use, the temperature of the solution, the time of development, and even the agitation used during development.

FILM SPEED

Film, of course, is available in a variety of speeds, expressed as ISO numbers, that indicate the film's relative sensitivity to light. The most commonly used black-and-white film speeds are ISO 100 (or 125) and 400, although slower and much faster speeds are available, too. There are also special-purpose films that offer extreme sharpness (at the cost of speed), as well as those that produce very-high-contrast subject rendition. Most black-and-white films are extremely flexible. Unlike the majority of color-negative films, which are subject to rigid processing procedures, you can alter the contrast of black-and-white negatives by using different developers or different dilutions of developers, or by increasing and decreasing developing time and/or temperature. You'll find instructions in film packages, or you can obtain technical sheets from the manufacturers.

You can also push film—raise its exposure index (EI)—to higher speeds and pull film—decrease exposure times for contrast control—by development control. Keep in mind that pushing can increase a film's contrast and grain. In fact, some films should be rated at higher or lower speeds according to the developer used. All of these possibilities make for a very versatile medium, one that you can tailor to your needs and individual shooting sessions. (By the way, EI is used when a film is rated at speeds other than what is indicated on the package.) As you work with exposure and development times with different films, you'll begin to see how changing one of the variables affects results. Testing is an excellent way to discover what works best for you.

The sensitivity of a film depends in large part on the size of the individual silver-halide crystals in the emulsion. The larger the area each crystal presents, the greater its light-capturing ability. Modern film technology has substantially reduced this speed/grain ratio and has made the capturing of light more efficient, but it still holds true that the faster the film the larger the grain in the final image. This is visible as enlargement size increases, and really becomes apparent when super-fast film speeds, those above ISO 1000, are used.

FILM TYPES

There are dozens of black-and-white films on the market today. Speeds range from ISO 25 to EI 3200. Films with similar speeds from different manufacturers might have slightly finer grain structures and be somewhat sharper than others, but each has its own special charms. Film with an ISO 100 speed is sharper and less grainy than an ISO 400 film; however, the faster film allows for more leeway in low-light shooting situations and when you want to set narrower apertures and/or faster shutter speeds for handheld shooting. For example, Agfapan 25 is exquisitely sharp and fine-grained, yet in many situations, its speed precludes shooting without a tripod. And if you want very high grain or other special effects, try Kodak Recording Film; this is an ISO 1000 emulsion that can be enlarged for a very gritty effect.

Black-and-white films come in both amateur and professional emulsions. Sometimes the major difference between the two is that the professional emulsion has a layer that provides "tooth" for retouching, such as removing blemishes from portraits. Some of the professional films require special handling and developing. If you deviate too far from the recommendations, you'll get a difficult-to-print negative. In general, the amateur versions are a bit more "forgiving," but this doesn't mean that you can be careless when processing. As you work with all these films, you'll get a feel for what is best for your type of images. The secret to success with all films is to test, test, and then test some more. Only trial and error can teach you what works well for you.

Underexposure/Underdevelopment: Much of the tonal information isn't recorded, and even the bright highlights are weak here.

Underexposure/Overdevelopment: Contrast has picked up and highlight areas are denser, but shadow detail is still weak.

Normal Exposure/Normal Development: Shadow detail is evident with strong but printable highlights.

Overexposure/Overdevelopment: The entire image has picked up density, but highlights are quite hot and might be difficult to print.

Overexposure/Underdevelopment: The overall density on the negative is reduced, but it is still more contrasty, and thus more difficult to print, than the normal exposure/normal development negative.

Although you might not be able to "rescue" exposure and developing mistakes, learning to identify where the problem lies can help you to create better negatives in the future. Reading negatives is an essential part of this, and experience is the best guide. One way to learn how to read negatives and to train your eye is to create a catalog of negative types that you can use as a reference later. Find a scene with a good brightness range and shoot bracket sequences of plus and minus three stops on one roll of 36-exposure ISO 400 black-and-white film. Then cut the film into thirds in the darkroom, and develop one-third of it normally, develop one-third 50 percent longer, and develop one-third 30 percent shorter. What you will have created is basically every exposure/development combination possible, as shown here. (Photos © Grace Schaub)

PROCESSING BLACK-AND-WHITE FILM

There is no point in getting involved with your own printing unless you—or a very trusted lab—handles your negative developing. Too much rides on the results of your work for you to leave processing in the hands of a standard photofinisher or drugstore. If you have any doubts about this, try an experiment. Send a few rolls of the same scene to a number of different labs. I guarantee that you'll be astonished at the variations in density, cleanliness, and overall printability.

The processing instruction sheet packed with film tells you to develop for, suppose, 8 minutes at 68° F. The instructions outline an agitation schedule and advise on adjusting times for variations in temperature. While following these instructions should yield printable negatives, they don't necessarily result in optimum negatives for every individual. In some cases, the times and temperatures given are an average, and only through testing can you arrive at what is most appropriate for you. In fact, you might have to modify your developing technique to achieve the most printable negatives for your style of printing.

The first step in gaining control over your negatives is knowing the look of the negative you want to produce. Some printers like *dense* negatives, which are slightly overdeveloped and/or overexposed; others prefer *thin* negatives, which are slightly underexposed and/or underdeveloped. This partiality is based on a number of factors, including the type of light source a darkroom worker prints with. Generally, those printing with a condenser-type head prefer slightly thinner negatives, while those who work with a cold-light head prefer denser negatives. These preferences are valid, but they are too often subjective and can't be quantified or qualified by graphs and charts. The point is to be able to reach your goal

consistently and to be able to produce the kind of negative you want without having to resort to luck. Start with the basics, and get your procedures down cold. Once you accomplish this, you can begin to make subtle alterations in your prints as needed.

A good way to introduce yourself to how exposure and development affect results is to run a series of tests. Shoot the same scene with three rolls of different conventional films, such as Tri-X, HP-5 Plus, or Agfapan 400. Bracket exposures two stops higher and lower than your averaged reading on each roll. For example, suppose the reading is $f/8$ for $1/125$ sec. A bracketed sequence for this reading would be $f/4$, $f/5.6$, $f/8$, $f/11$ and $f/16$, all for $1/125$ sec. Develop the first roll of film for the recommended time, the second roll at about 20 percent less than the recommended time, and the third roll at about 30 percent more than the recommended time.

Next, make *contact sheets* (see page 64), and study the negatives. This test will give you a reference catalog of all the variables and how they affect results. It will also help you trace mistakes in the future. You'll see negatives that are: overexposed and overdeveloped, overexposed and underdeveloped, underexposed and overdeveloped, underexposed and underdeveloped, as well as normally exposed and developed. You might also want to make study prints of the various types of negatives and see how tonal reproduction and contrast are affected by exposure and processing. Testing in this manner can be a revelation.

As already discussed, proper exposure and development yield easily printable negatives. They also provide you with the most leeway in making a wide range of interpretive printing decisions. Of course, at times you might have to print a problem negative. There are ways to handle these problems. The next step is to start printing, beginning with contact sheets, or proof sheets, of the negatives.

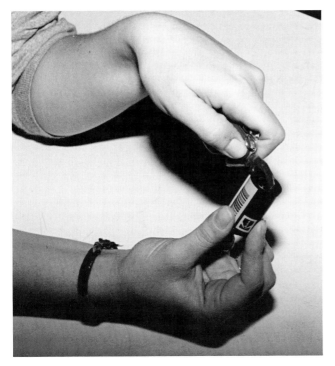

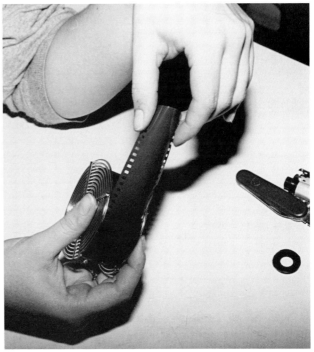

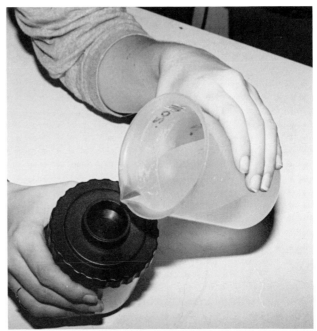

The first step in 35mm film processing is getting the film out of the cassette, as seen in the shot above on the left. Use a bottle opener to pry off the end cap—in total darkness, of course. After you get the film out of the cassette, cut the film from the plastic retainer. Next, cut a half-moon shape in the leader, hold the rolled-up film in one hand, and begin to load it onto the reel, as shown in the picture above on the right. Once you have the film on the reel, place it inside the film tank and cover the tank with the lid, as the shot

directly above on the left shows. At this point, you can carry out the other processing steps in normal room light. Film-tank lids have both a lip that enables you to add and drain solutions in normal room light and a cover. In the picture directly above on the right, the developer is added to the tank. After you add the solutions, replace the cover, and then follow the time and agitation procedure. After the developer step, drain the solution and proceed to the short-stop and fixer baths, and washing.

MAKING CONTACT SHEETS

Once you've developed and dried your film, you'll probably be eager to see the results. When you've gained enough experience, you can "read" the negatives by holding them up to the light or placing them down on a lightbox and viewing each frame through a loupe. But even experienced photographers prefer to see a contact sheet, or proof sheet, of their shoot right away. A contact sheet is a print of the entire roll of film. It shows you a positive image of the negative that you can use to check composition, subject matter, and, to a certain extent, the range of tones you have captured on film. Generally, the contact is made on sheets of 8 x 10 paper; an entire roll of 36-exposure 35mm film can take up two sheets, while a roll of 12-exposure 120 film can fit on one. You can also fit four 4 x 5 negatives or two 5 x 7 negatives on this same sheet size. For 35mm negatives, cut the roll of film into six equal strips of six exposures each; cut the 120 roll of film in strips according to format.

MATERIALS NEEDED

In order to make a contact print, you'll need, of course, a contact-printing frame. This is made of a piece of glass hinged to a printing platform, which is usually covered with a foam or semi-soft support. Some contact-printing frames also come with a latch that, when closed, makes a snug fit of the negative/paper/glass sandwich. These latches are essential if the glass is lightweight because a poor fit might cause an unsharp print resulting from poor contact between the negatives and paper. You can easily build a contact-printing frame; just be sure that the edges of the glass are sanded down or heavily taped.

Before you can process the exposed prints, you'll have to prepare your chemistry. Set up four trays; these can be 8 x 10, 11 x 14, or whatever size you use. The first tray receives the print developer. If you haven't already done so, mix a working solution by following the instructions on the package. The second tray holds the short stop or the water bath. The third tray should hold the fixing bath. The last tray should contain water with a circulating washer; you might also want to use a wash-aid and a final wash for quicker processing times if you're printing on FB paper. Once you set up the trays, turn out the white lights and turn on the enlarger and safelights.

Contact prints can be made on either FB or RC paper stock. Many people find the RC papers satisfactory since they offer quick turnaround in processing, washing, and drying. In truth, there's little advantage in making contact proofs on FB papers. You can also make enlarged proof sheets, a projection printing setup in which the negatives are placed in a glass negative carrier and enlarged on one sheet of, for example, 11 x 14 paper. To do this properly without cutting the 35mm negatives into very small snippets, you'll need a 4 x 5 enlarger; cut the film in strips of three and put three strips in a glass carrier and enlarge. Custom labs often offer this processing service.

You'll probably want to make your contact sheets on a "normal" contrast grade of paper, such as a #2 grade. If you're printing on a VC paper with a condenser light source, you'll end up with about the same contrast grade; a cold-light source yields a slightly higher contrast on unfiltered VC paper. So why print on a #2 grade? In order to check the tonal values, you'll want to print on a normal grade #2 paper, one that displays the entire range of what the negative has to offer. Printing on a higher grade compresses the scale somewhat, while a lower grade might not display the full richness of your images. Higher deviations from the norm, such as #0 and #4 grades, yield a more radical rendition altogether (see page 112).

However, even though you print on a normal grade of paper and get pretty close to the optimum printing time for an individual frame, the contact sheet serves only as an indication of the potential of an image. As such, it is a starting point for your considerations of what you can do in making the final print. It also serves as a record of your shooting, one that should be stored along with your negatives in your files.

THE STEP-BY-STEP PROCEDURE

Making a contact print is easy. First, place the contact-printing frame under the enlarger. Then put a negative carrier in the enlarger, turn on the focusing light, and raise the enlarger until the entire frame is covered with light. Don't focus the light because any specks of dust or lint on the condenser glass will probably show up in the print. When that is set, turn off the light and place an 8 x 10 sheet of paper emulsion side up (with glossy paper, the shiny side; with matte paper, the side that curls inward or, if the paper is flat, the side that is cooler to the touch) onto the base of the opened frame. Place the negatives in number order (strip 1 through 6 on top, then 7 through 12, and so forth) onto the paper emulsion side down. When the negatives are in place, carefully close the glass cover and latch the sandwich into place.

One problem with this procedure is that when you encounter negatives with excessive curl, you place them down and they curl right back up, throwing off your attempt to put them neatly onto one sheet of paper. This often happens with thin-emulsion negatives and those that weren't dried with a weighted clip at the bottom. It can also occur if negatives weren't cut and stored in file sheets immediately after processing.

There are a number of solutions to this problem. One is to raise the glass slightly and slide the negatives in, allowing the back of the glass to catch and hold the strip upon insertion. This cumbersome process can lead to scratching if you're not very careful. However, experience will show you that it does indeed work. Another solution is to keep the negatives in the plastic file holder and contact-print them right through it. Of course, this will cause some unsharpness in the proof sheet because you're keeping the negatives from coming in direct contact with the printing paper. However, this can be preferable to pushing and pulling the delicate negatives into the frame.

Another alternative is to purchase a contact-printing frame with retaining bands that hold individual negative strips. Ribbed frames are available for 35mm and 120 film; however, some reduce by one the number of strips you can place in the frame. Whatever solution is best for you, keep in mind that regardless of how carefully you process and file negatives, you'll have some curl in freshly processed film.

The amount of exposure you give a contact print depends on the density of the negatives, the speed of the printing paper, and the output of your enlarger's light source. Because you

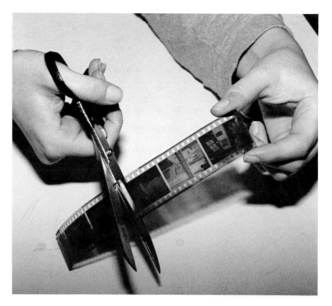

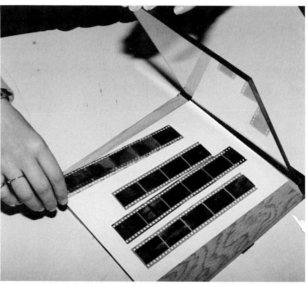

After the negatives are dry, cut them into strips of four, five, or six frames, as shown above. The number of frames depends on the film format and the type of storage sleeve and contact print you want to make. The space between frames can be narrow, so be sure to cut carefully. Doing this over a lightbox can help you see the cut line better. To make a contact sheet, shown directly above, lay the negative strips emulsion side down onto your printing paper, which should be emulsion side up. Once you line up the negatives, lower the glass; this presses the negatives firmly against the paper, ensuring sharp images.

aren't projection printing, the exposure time will usually be shorter than that needed for making enlargements. Suppose you make an exposure with an f/5.6 aperture on your enlarging lens. Contact printing exposure time on a relatively fast paper can run from 1 to 10 seconds. How do you determine the exact printing time? Make a *test print*. Once you have the sandwich in place, set the lens to f/5.6 and cover the entire frame with a piece of opaque cardboard. Set your timer to 2 seconds, uncover one-fifth of the frame, and expose. Then uncover the next fifth, and expose for the same interval; do the same with the entire frame uncovered.

Once you process your print, you'll see the effect of 2-, 4-, 6-, 8- and 10-second exposure times. If the print needs more exposure, it will be light and lack full image information; if it comes up too quickly in the developer and is too dark when processing is complete, it requires less exposure time. Check to see which portion yields the best results, with full picture information, and expose an entire new sheet accordingly. With experience and by using the same paper for contacts, you'll be able to estimate the best contact printing times just by looking at the negatives.

However, negatives on the same roll of film made at different times under different lighting conditions might have quite different densities, thereby requiring different exposures for best results. This is quite common with 35mm rolls of film, especially when the photographer's metering isn't exactly accurate. If this happens, make two contact sheets, one at a longer and the other at a shorter exposure time. Doing this will help you get a better "read" of the entire roll of film.

MAKING A CONTACT PRINT

1. Cut the dried negatives into strips that will fit onto an 8 x 10 sheet of paper.

2. Place the empty negative carrier in the enlarger; raise the enlarger to the height at which the light covers the entire contact-printing frame, and then refocus the light.

3. Place the printing paper emulsion side up into the contact-printing frame; place the negatives emulsion side down onto the paper, and then close the printing frame.

4. Expose (test exposure times).

5. Process the print.

6. Dry the print, and store it with the negatives.

Proof sheets enable you to catalog and file your images easily. They also serve as preliminary test prints for composition, exposure, and sharpness, although you usually need to closely inspect the negatives in order to make the best judgement. This proof sheet of a 10-exposure 6 x 7 120 format film was made on a single piece of 8 x 10 paper.

The negatives used for this series were quite contrasty but have produced some very good images. To prove the point, a proof sheet was first made on a #4 paper and underexposed, as seen on the far left. This makes the roll look like a disaster. The next set, shown on the left, was made on the same paper but with more exposure time. The negatives still look poor. However, when a proof sheet was made on a #1 paper, as seen on the right, the printability of the negatives is revealed and the images are much easier to read. Always note the contrast grade used for making proofs on the back of the paper; this can save you some printing time later. (Photos © Grace Schaub)

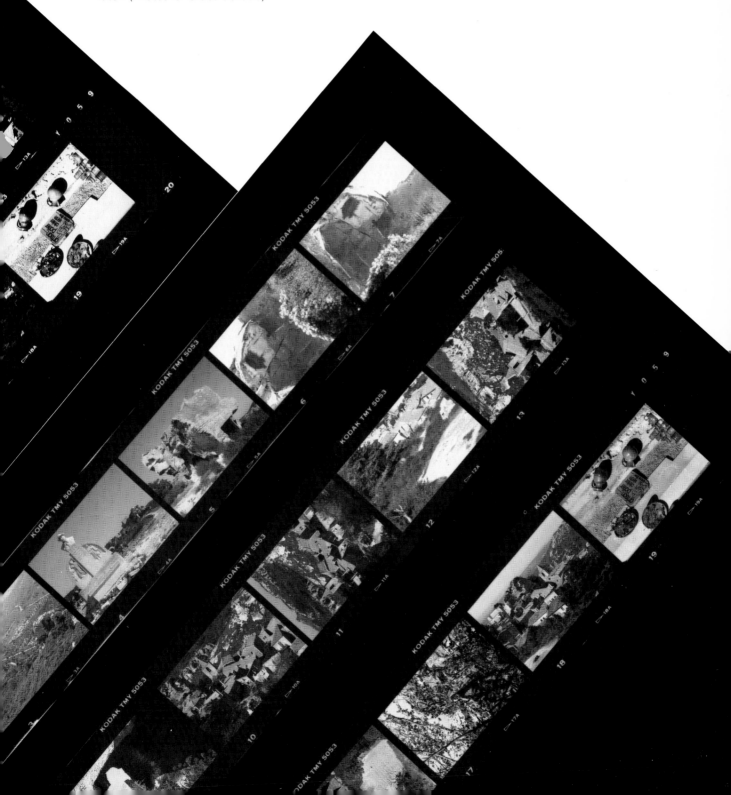

PART FOUR

PREPARING TO PRINT

Once you decide which images to print, you have to make some basic choices about how you want the image to look on paper. This includes such considerations as how large you want to make the image, whether you want to print the image full frame or to crop it, and if the image would look better on a warm- or cold-tone paper. You then have other important variables to consider, including image contrast, print density, and adding or subtracting light from select parts of the image.

While these might seem daunting, you simply have to understand how each element can affect the final image and then apply that knowledge to making a print that best communicates your feelings about the subject. Although many of these options are discussed here, there is no substitute for experimentation and testing on your part.

Don't be surprised if these decisions change over time. Many experienced printers find that they go through stages: printing "down," or dark, during one stage of their work, and printing "up," or high key, during another. The art you produce can indicate how you relate to the world at any given time. That is both the beauty of this craft and the reason why printing your own images can be so rewarding.

MAKING PRINTING DECISIONS

One of the best ways to understand how an effective print looks is to study the work of photographer/printmakers who have mastered the craft. Go to museums, gallery shows, and small art dealers that have a sampling of work you admire. If a print "grabs" you, try to understand what it is about the work that makes you stop and study it. Of course, the subject matter is important, but look beyond that to study how the craftsperson has used printing technique as an essential part of the overall communication of the image. Is a full tonal scale (from white through the gray scale to black) essential, or is a high or low contrast rendition an important part of the effect? Is there a high, stark contrast at work, or is there a diffuse feeling to the image? Are shadow areas deep and dark, or are details revealed in the subtle distinction between the darker tones? Is light rendition believable, or is there a tricky, experimental vision at work? Although books and monographs are excellent ways to acquaint yourself with the work of a number of different photographers, nothing quite matches the impact of seeing an actual print before you. Regardless of how well a book is printed, the actual print is always a generation away from the printed page.

When you first begin printing, you might find it difficult to decide which approach to take. Should you go for as full a tonal scale as possible, or should you alter contrast and go for a graphic, or even softer version of the scene? Should you print on a "warm" or "cold" paper, and should toning be used? I suggest starting out by making a straight print and getting into special effects as you go along. This will give you a firm foundation in printmaking—one you can build on as you gain experience.

In large part, form should follow function; let the subject matter guide you on your way. For example, if you have an urban scene dominated by steel and glass, you might find that a high-contrast rendition does the job best. Conversely, if you have a nature scene through which you want to evoke a romanticized version of reality, perhaps a soft contrast and a warm-toned paper combination will be best. In truth, there are no set rules, and you might find that you base your decisions more upon how you feel when you're printing than on a dictum laid down here or elsewhere.

One of the best aids in making these decisions is making up a printing "catalog," which is a series of images of different subjects with a wide range of papers and contrasts. Select one image from a number of different "types," such as a nature scene, an urban image, a portrait, and an abstract. When you're printing with a specific set of developers and papers, take the time to pull out these "archetypes" first and to make a work print. Indicate on the back the print paper, contrast grade, developer, and the steps used, and file it away in a folder. Then, when it comes time to make those printing decisions, review your file for guidelines. Although this won't be a cure-all and your decisions might be more emotional than academic, it can give you a good overview of the possibilities in the beginning.

CHOOSING FORMAT AND ENLARGEMENT SIZES

Negatives can be printed in any number of ways; you can make contact prints, reduce them, or enlarge them as you see fit. How big or small you make a print depends on several factors, including negative sharpness, subject matter, and the end use of the print itself. Also, you're not limited to the original proportions of the negative in the printed image; although you start out with a rectangular or square format, you can crop as you wish and change a horizontal to a vertical, or turn a 3 x 5 negative ratio into a 3 x 10 composition (see page 74 for more information on cropping).

Commercially available printing paper is sold in a number of standard sizes, including 4 x 5, 5 x 7, 8 x 10, 11 x 14, 16 x 20, and 20 x 24 inches. While you can print right to the edges of the paper, I find it best to print inside the outer dimensions; this allows some room for inset borders, handling, and trimming if I decide to mount the print later. For example, I'll print 6 x 9 inches on an 8 x 10 paper; and 8 x 12 inches on an 11 x 14 paper. But even before you set about printing, you have to decide just what size enlargement fits a particular shot.

The first step is to determine just how much enlarging a given negative can take. Place your selected negative in the carrier, and raise the

Just as a self-made negative catalog can help you identify negative types, a print diary that illustrates various paper/developer combinations and printing techniques can come in handy when you decide what to use for a particular image. I often use this image of a tree in a forest when I test a new paper or paper/developer combination. These images are from my paper catalog.

I used a #3 neutral-to-cold-tone paper and Dektol mixed 1:2 for this image. The result is a bit hard, but it has good blacks and a feeling of crispness.

Here, I used a #1 matte paper and Dektol mixed 1:1. The picture has some extra snap from the concentrated developer, which can be good for a low-key image.

To produce this image, I chose a #2 warm-tone matte paper and Selectol mixed 1:2. The picture has an open feeling and contains both good shadow detail and excellent warm tones.

enlarger to the desired height. Then check image sharpness. If the image becomes unsharp, lower the enlarger until it becomes sharper. The next step is to consider grain. Naturally, the bigger the enlargement, the grainier it looks. If you have a fairly grainy rendition at 8 x 10, grain will certainly be obvious as you continue to increase the size of the print. I don't find grain objectionable, but if you do, it'll become a major factor in determining enlargement size. Grain can be de-emphasized somewhat by printing on a lower-contrast paper or by using a diffusion enlarger head, but neither of these might meet the needs of the image itself.

The main consideration in enlargement size should be the subject of the picture. In some cases, the power of the image will overcome any of these considerations. Generally, some images lend themselves to big prints; others call for a more intimate approach. This is an individual—and personal—matter. However, don't think that a picture must be big in order to have impact. If you find that you always need to make big prints to make an impression, you should rethink your subject matter and question your motivation. An image should stand on its own, regardless of size. All a big print does is make the viewer stand back a bit more to study it. If it is a solid image, it will be fine even as small as 5 x 7.

The end use of the print is an important consideration, too. For example, if you're printing for standard publication, use an 8 x 10 because this is the size most printing houses are accustomed to working with. Also, if the print is being down-sized in the final publication, the resolution and quality won't be diminished as they would be if the size were increased from, for example, a 3 x 5 to an 8 x 10. If you're printing for a gallery show, let your subject matter be your guide. Too many people feel that they have to make large prints for a show, but this isn't necessary. I've seen very effective and beautiful 5 x 7 prints hung for a show; the more intimate presentation can work wonders. Large or small, do what is comfortable and fitting.

Of course, the negative size from which you're printing will dramatically affect how large the print can be made. Making a 16 x 20 print from a 4 x 5 negative requires much less enlargement than does the same size print from a 35mm negative, which translates to more sharpness and less grain. In general, you'll find it very difficult to match print quality between 35mm and large-format negatives.

Finally, film speed and quality influence how far you can go and still have an effective print. Some films are simply sharper and finer-grained than others. Also, how you expose and develop the negative will have a profound influence on enlargement quality. A poorly handled negative will never yield anything approaching that of one that has been well exposed and processed.

CROPPING

Every time you take a picture, you crop. Putting the world into a frame is part of the art of photography, and a great image is often separated from an adequate one by the way in which you choose to frame the subject matter. However, there might be times when your composition is less than ideal; perhaps you couldn't get close enough or some element, seen only when you view your contact sheets, throws off the whole picture. This is where cropping—finding the frame within the frame— comes to the rescue. Although it won't solve all of your compositional problems, it can be useful in shaping up many images. Of course, the degree to which you can crop depends on the various enlargement factors. Crop too much, and you might go beyond the limits of good print quality.

Be aware that when you meet other printers, you'll hear two schools of thought on this issue. First, some feel that cropping is a sin, that it intrudes on the photographer's vision at the moment when the shutter was snapped. Others think that printing gives you the leeway to create images that are part of a process that includes cropping for the best effect.

Cropping can be used for both image correction and enhancement. An example of image correction is straightening a horizon line. Here, you position your print easel so that the line in the image is parallel to the bottom of the paper. Of course, this means that you'll have to crop to eliminate some of the corners of the image. You also crop whenever you print a 35mm film on a full 8 x 10 sheet of paper; some of the edges are eliminated. Of course, you can print full frame on an 8 x 10 paper with a 35mm negative, but you'll have extra white space on the top and/or bottom of the print.

Cropping eliminates extraneous information that might hinder the effectiveness of the image. Getting the right spot for this picture was difficult because other photographers had staked claims by the time I arrived. I shot anyway, knowing that I could crop later as needed. The picture shown above is the full frame; the picture on the left is the cropped image from the same negative.

In the scene on the right, which I came upon in Paris, the man moved before I had a chance to get in closer. So the only frame I had of the scene was filled with extraneous material. The picture I "saw" was the one shown below, and it defined the way I cropped when making the final print.

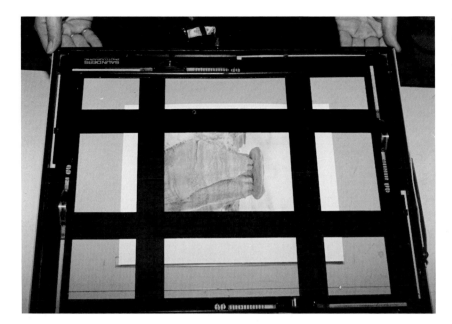

This bladed easel is ideal for cropping; you can readily adjust it until you see the desired framing of the image.

When you crop for enhancement, you're using the enlarger as you do a zoom lens. There are limits to this technique because of the size of the original negative and the speed and grain structure of the film. Extreme cropping may result in a serious loss of image quality. Many times, you might want to convert a horizontal to a vertical, or vice versa.

You can determine how to crop by consulting your contact sheet, or by making a full-frame print and playing with two pieces of right-angle boards. Moving the boards in and around the image can lead to some fascinating alternatives. Once you decide on the cropping—on the proof sheet or work print—draw the outlines with a grease pencil, keeping in mind that you might have to adjust the borders according to the format of the print you want to make. You can also make *cropping templates*. These are windows within standard-size boards that correspond to the height-to-width ratios of the final prints.

Of course, there is no reason to always echo the size of the printing paper on hand. A 3 x 10 print can be as effective as a more conventional size; however, make sure that the cropping enhances the subject and isn't just a superficial effect. If you find that you're always cropping images, examine your shooting techniques. You might have to get closer to your subject, buy a telephoto lens, or think more about composition before you snap the shutter. Remember, when you print your own pictures, you'll become a better photographer.

FOCUSING

There is no point taking the time to shoot a sharp picture if your negatives aren't focused properly when you enlarge. Proper focus starts with taking care of your enlarger and extends to how you focus the image on the easel. Focusing is a key element in enlarging, so understanding it step by step is vital. Once you've checked the enlarger alignment, cleaned the negative, and placed it in the enlarger, adjust the height of the enlarger head for the size enlargement you wish to make. Eyeball a rough focus, and lock the enlarger by tightening the knobs. (Some enlargers have tension bands and don't have to be tightened down.) Make sure that the lens is wide open (set to the maximum aperture) because this allows the most light through.

Next, place a sheet of paper as thick as the one you're printing on in the easel. You won't be processing this sheet; it's simply a focusing sheet that ensures that the plane of focus will be on the paper surface, not the easel surface. In fact, you can save this sheet for all future printing of papers of similar thicknesses. Start by placing the grain focuser in the middle of the print and take a look at the print through the eyepiece. At first you might see an indistinct "fuzz," but as you turn the fine-focusing knob on the enlarger you'll see this fuzz change dramatically to actual clumps of grain. Just a slight turn will make a major difference.

After you see distinct grain in your eyepiece, move as far to the edges of the print as the focuser will allow. If you have to make an

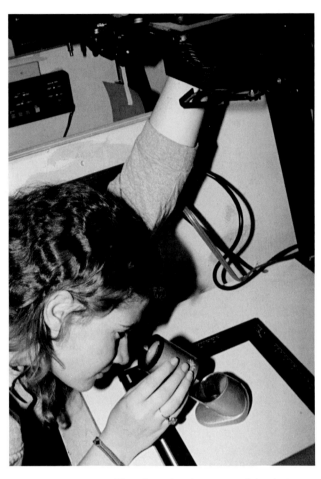

Fine focusing is accomplished via a grain magnifier. This printer uses her left hand to adjust the enlarger's fine-focusing knob while her eye is trained on the grain of the image—not the picture—as seen in the grain focuser's viewing glass, as shown above on the right. When the grain is completely sharp, as shown on the right, the image is in focus.

extensive adjustment, go back to the center and focus again. Too much of a difference might signal an alignment problem or a negative pop (see below for more about eliminating negative popping). Go back and forth until the entire print is sharp.

Next, close the lens down to the printing aperture; in most cases, this will be about f/8. As with most lenses, the best resolving power is available at or close to the middle aperture numbers. However, you might have to use a different aperture to increase or decrease printing times. This will depend on the density of the negative, the speed of the paper, and the amount of handwork a negative requires. Usually, you can aim for printing times between 10 and 25 seconds. Also, if you notice a slight alignment problem or negative curl, you can compensate by closing the lens down to a smaller aperture.

One problem you might run into is *negative popping* during the focusing and enlarging steps. This is not a factor when you use glass carriers, although, as discussed earlier, these must be kept scrupulously clean. The heat from the enlarger head (especially condenser enlargers) can cause the negative to shift during the focusing/exposure sequence; this moves the negative out of the plane of focus and might cause what you thought was a well-focused image to become unsharp. One way to combat negative popping is to install a heat-absorbing filter between the lamp housing and negative stage. Many enlargers have a special filter drawer in the head in which you can place this glass. While this reduces the amount of heat, you might still have a problem.

You can also "pre-pop" the negative using a red filter attached via a turn mount beneath the lens on the enlarger. (If you don't have one, you can purchase one and attach it later.) Before you take the paper out, turn on the enlarger for about 30 seconds to pre-warm the negative. In the meantime, you can focus and set up the easel. Once this is done and with the enlarger lamp still on, swing the red filter under the lens (the red filter makes the paper "blind" to the light so that no exposure is made), place your paper in the easel, briefly turn off the enlarger light, swing the filter out of the way, and hit the timer button to make the exposure. This process might sound difficult but it becomes second nature after a while. Also, it might not be

necessary if you don't have a chronic negative-popping problem. This also might not be necessary with a cold-light head since its operating temperature is considerably lower than that of condenser-head enlargers.

Once you've focused the negative, remove the focusing sheet from the easel, replace it with your enlarging paper, and begin printing procedures. While this might seem to be an inordinate number of steps, it does guarantee edge-to-edge sharpness in prints.

MATCHING NEGATIVES TO CONTRAST GRADE

As already mentioned, you can print on a wide variety of contrast-grade papers ranging from #0 to #5. A "normal" (standard) grade of paper is #2 and yields a full range of tones from a well-exposed and properly developed negative. A #0 paper yields a very low-contrast rendition of a negative, while a #5 yields a very high-contrast one. Generally, your negatives should be printed on a #2 or #3 paper, depending upon the light source with which you enlarge for a straight print. Here, you want to match the densities actually recorded on the negative to those on the final print. However, sometimes you might want to alter the rendition of a scene for emotional purposes, or to use a high- or low-contrast paper to try to squeeze more information from an over- or underexposed negative.

Reading negatives—understanding which contrast grade is best for the image at hand— is one of the main challenges of printing. Although experience is, of course, the best teacher, you can also refer to the negative exposure/development tests discussed on page 62. For the most part, you can get more information from an underexposed negative by printing it on a #3 or #4 contrast paper. Although increasing contrast causes the loss of some image information in the deep shadows and bright highlights, it can give the overall image a needed boost. Conversely, if you have a high-contrast negative, especially one in which the highlights are very dense and print as "paper white," you can choose a low-contrast paper to help control those highlights. However, low-contrast papers might not always give you rich blacks. Their makeup is such that the best you might get is a deep gray. This is the price of extreme low contrast.

When you have a low-contrast negative like the one shown on the right, you can either keep the original values or boost the contrast as needed. The resulting differences can be quite dramatic, as shown in the #2 contrast-grade selection shown directly below and the #4 version of this scene shown on the bottom of the page.

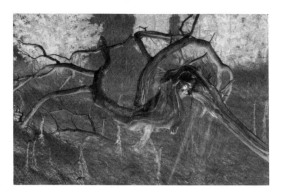

When a negative is contrasty, you might have trouble with the highlights and be forced to control them by printing on a lower-than-normal contrast grade. The negative shown on the left is fine except for the burned-up highlight areas. When printed on a #3 paper (to illustrate the point), as shown directly below, the highlight areas are very harsh and the shadow areas lose all separation. Although I could have tried to burn in those highlights, the twists and turns of the branches would have made this difficult. One way to avoid this problem is to print on a lower-contrast-grade paper. A print made on a #1 paper, shown on the bottom of the page, controls the highlights and opens up detail in the shadows.

The negative shown on the right, exposed on a bright summer day in the south of France, typifies the contrast problems of midday shooting. When highlights are this burnt-up, the only solution, other than a long process of burning and dodging, is to print using a low-contrast paper or using a low-contrast filter with VC paper. These prints were made on #1 and #4 paper. Each print was exposed to give the highlights texture without burning in; in other words, these were printed for highlight values. Note how the shadow detail disappears in the higher-contrast image. (Photos © Grace Schaub)

Juggling contrast grades for correcting poorly exposed or processed negatives can make the difference between your being able to make a satisfactory print or just a poor one. If you always have to print on a high- or low-contrast paper, or with high- or low-contrast filters with VC paper, you have a developing and/or exposure problem. You should correct it as soon as possible.

A more creative approach to matching contrast grade papers to negatives is used for enhancing the mood or feeling of an image. For example, if you shot a foggy morning or a portrait of someone bathed in soft window light, rather than always print on a normal paper, you might opt for a low-contrast grade to enhance the nuances in either subject's tonal scale. Or if you have an image of city buildings reaching into the sky, you might want to bring out the hardness of the glass and steel sky-scrapers by printing on a high-contrast grade. This paper will render it in bold values: deep blacks and bright highlights.

But before you can make these decisions, you need to train yourself to read the negative itself and to be able to predict how paper selection will affect the appearance of the print. Use an 8X loupe to inspect the negative, and look at the varying tones, or densities. Watch for detail in the thinner portions of the negative. Also, check to see if there is texture, or separation among the highlight values. Find a negative that has a good range of tones, and print it on a range of contrast-grade papers. Similarly, print thin and thick negatives on all grades. Once you get a feel for matching negative quality with contrast grades, as well as how to play the game of corrective and enhancement printing, you'll have learned a great deal about this craft.

MAKING TEST PRINTS

Just as a negative with a full range of tones has the best potential to translate into a quality print, a print needs proper exposure and development to yield the best quality the paper offers. A good straight print combines the proper density and contrast. If a print is too light, a result of too little exposure in the enlarger or underdevelopment in the tray, essential details will be lost. In addition, the highlights will be as light as the paper base. A print that is too dark, usually because of overexposure in the enlarger, will also lose details, but in the shadow areas of the image. You might see these details in the negative, but overexposure causes them to become lost.

A good print has deep blacks, yet still shows all the important image details in both the highlights and shadows. (Again, this applies only to straight printing; interpretive printing can be another matter.) This also holds for paper contrast, where proper matching of negative to paper contrast grade should aid in reproducing nearly all of the tones available in the negative. Some tonal compression occurs when you go from a negative to any print, although losing too much in the process is the sign of poor printing techniques.

Most beginning printers tend to make prints with too much contrast, thinking that the extra snap enhances the image. However, this desire for snap should be replaced with an appreciation of tones and tonal continuity. Try for bright highlights with a tone just below paper white, deep blacks, and as full a range of middle grays as possible. Again, start by making good straight prints, and interpretive work will follow naturally.

The test print helps you determine the exposure and contrast grade needed to achieve this tonal richness—without endless trial and error. Here is how to do it. First, place the negative in the carrier, then frame and focus the image, and, finally, set your lens to the proper printing aperture. You'll be exposing in "bursts" of a few seconds duration each, and accumulating time as you move a cover sheet along the print. Set your timer for a short duration of, for example, 3 seconds. Most timers have a function that automatically resets for the same time after you expose.

Next, choose the paper that you think will match the negative. If you're not sure which contrast grade to use, start with a #2, or put a #2 filter in place with VC paper. Place the paper in the easel, and cover 80 percent of it with a cover sheet. Make sure the cover sheet is opaque because you don't want light coming through it to affect exposure time. Expose for the first burst. Move the cover sheet along, being careful not to nudge the print in the easel out of position, and then allow 20 percent or so of the total paper size to be uncovered with each subsequent exposure.

When making test-strip prints, use an opaque board to create the separate exposure strips. After each exposure burst, reveal another section of the printing paper by moving the board an inch or two down the length of the paper. Keep the sections as equal in size as possible, and try to get a minimum of five exposure strips on each sheet of paper.

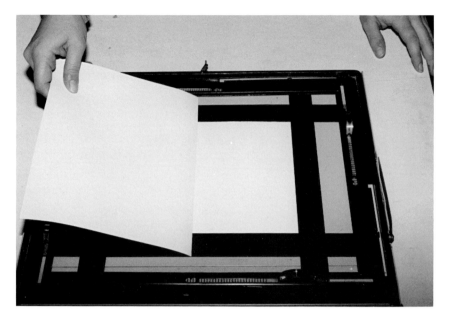

Try to get about five separate exposures onto a sheet of paper. In this example, this will give you exposure times of 3, 6, 9, 12, and 15 seconds. Run the print through the regular processing procedure—develop, stop, and fix—and let it rinse in a water bath for a minute or two. Many people try to judge their prints in the amber-lit darkroom. Seasoned printers can get away with this, but you'll find that you get better results if you begin by inspecting the print in white light. To do this, either secure your paper and turn on the lights in the darkroom or take the print out to where you can view it in white light.

If all the strips are too light or too dark, you'll need to make a new test-strip print. If the strips are too dark, decrease the duration of the burst or stop down the lens one stop. Conversely, if all of the strips are too light, increase the burst duration or open up the lens one stop. Be aware that prints have a tendency to "dry down," which means that they look slightly more contrasty when wet than when dry. Experience will show you how to evaluate and compensate for this effect.

Once you've arrived at a good selection of well-exposed test strips, take a look at the one or two strips that seem to bring out the best in the image. Then check for the best exposure time to see if the contrast grade you've selected brings out the best in the image. Check the highlight and shadow areas; if there is good

detail in both, as well as deep blacks, then you've already found the most effective exposure time and selected the best contrast paper for the image. You might have to adjust the exposure time by 1 or 2 seconds, but this is a minor consideration.

Make a checklist for yourself. Is the exposure time you've chosen making the print too light or too dark? Is the contrast making the image look too flat or too harsh? Suppose you have an exposure strip where the blacks are rich and deep, yet the whites don't have texture and look washed out. This indicates that you should use a lower contrast grade or filter. Conversely, suppose the strip has good texture in the whites, but the blacks have a muddy, grayish appearance. Here, a higher-contrast grade is needed. Note that switching contrast grades might necessitate exposure compensation, depending on the paper you use.

Once you have a strip that gives you good exposure and contrast, make a full test print at the selected time and grade. This will validate your test and reveal if you have to do handwork before achieving a finished print. You'll see parts of the image that weren't covered by the selected time and contrast tests and get information on burning and dodging (see pages 88–91). Once you master this testing procedure, you should be able to make prints with a minimum of testing and paper waste. You won't have to get a good print through trial and error.

With test-strip procedures, you might be able to make a good print using as few as three sheets of paper if you can choose the appropriate contrast grade on the first read of the negative. This picture is a test-strip print, with each strip signifying 2-second increases in exposure. The fourth strip, the 8-second exposure, shows good highlight rendition, deep blacks, and a range of gray tones.

TONAL SCALE

This consists of the range of tones that are reproduced in a print. Tones are the blacks, whites, and shades of gray available in black-and-white image-making. The first aim is to record these tones when you expose the negative, then to reproduce them as effectively as possible. In general, we should try to get as full a scale as you can on the negative, then to make further decisions about them when you print. You can't create information on the print that doesn't exist on the negative.

Begin by getting a sense of what a tone really is. When you expose black-and-white film, you're recording brightness values that exist in the scene. A bright area causes a stronger reaction in the film's emulsion than a darker area, thereby creating more density in the negative; this reads as a darker section on the negative. Conversely, a dark or shadow area in the scene creates less of a reaction in the emulsion, records with less density, and looks lighter on the negative. When you make prints, you reverse this scheme to recreate the brightness values in the original scene.

Of course, a negative records more than just bright and dark areas; there is a whole range, or scale, of tonal values in between. Some photographers refer to these values as zones numbered 1 through 10 (with 1 being black and 10 being white). As such, the tonal scale recorded on the negative defines the range of possibilities within the final print. If you have a broad scale of negative tones, or densities, there is a very good chance that you can generate the same on the print.

But even if you expose negatives correctly, you can still lose them easily when you process and print. Improper development (too little, too much, poor temperature control) or printing (too much or too little contrast, too short or long exposure time) will ruin the full tonal scale you might have recorded initially on the negative. When you lose tonal fidelity in a print, the highlights might all merge in a harsh white, and the shadows, or deep tonal separations, might combine into a dark mass. You might even compress the tonal scale so much that all the tones are rendered a flat gray, with little or no distinction between them. When you print for a full tonal scale, you bring out all the possibilities in the image.

But tones don't always have to cover the entire range. Sometimes you'll want to print high- or low-key—emphasizing the lighter or darker range, respectively—with vivid contrast, or in muted scale. Let the tonal scale of the print match the subject and mood. There is some inevitable loss when you translate a negative to a print, just as there might be some loss of tonal recording on the negative when the brightness value range exceeds the recording capabilities of the film. In addition, film "sees" somewhat differently than the human eye, and might indeed be colorblind to some tonal separations. For example, a blue sky might record lighter than you see it. You can overcome some of these problems by using filters when you shoot, such as a yellow or orange filter to deepen blue skies.

However, even with some of these built-in hindrances, you should maximize the materials you have on hand by paying attention to and learning about their limitations, as well as working in and around them. Once you do, you'll begin to see how the fullest possible tonal scale can be recorded and eventually brought to play in the print.

Black-and-white printing calls for working with a wide range of tones from black through dark to light grays, to white. A gray scale, shown on the far right, gives an indication of these tones. By placing a gray scale between a negative and a print, you can see how the densities on the negative translate to the positive. Being able to read the tones and visualizing how they will translate on a print will help you make good printing decisions and simplify your work considerably.

MANUAL PRINTING CONTROLS

After you have determined the proper overall exposure time and contrast for the negative, you may discover that certain areas of the print aren't reproducing with the tone you prefer. For example, some highlights might be too harsh and lack detail, or some shadow areas might be blocked up and lack separation. Fortunately, there are a number of ways for you to further enhance the print. This is accomplished by working with light for correction and creativity: by subtracting and adding exposure to select areas of the print. These techniques are called *dodging* and *burning-in*, respectively.

Before you consider how to apply these controls, recheck your test strips and determine whether another exposure time or contrast grade yields a better tonal scale. If all of these backup checks don't reveal the source of the problem, you might simply have a situation in which the overall scale may be just right, but the problem areas, such as very bright highlights or deep shadows fall outside its range. This is when dodging or burning in may help.

DODGING

Dodging occurs when you hold back the light from a specific portion of the negative while it is being projected onto the paper during exposure. Typical situations that call for dodging are when the principal subject is highly backlit and when a portion of a subject is obscured in a bothersome shadow, such as under the brim of a hat. In each case, the area to be dodged hasn't received enough exposure on the negative and has less density than the rest of the image. Whatever the reason, dodging is always used to help bring detail into shadow areas; it keeps those areas from receiving too much light and thus printing too dark.

The best dodging tool is a small piece of opaque board taped to the end of a flexible but sturdy wire. Use a very thin wire because a wire that is too thick might leave a mark (by creating a shadow on the print). Before you do your final print, practice a bit with the focusing light on. Place the end of the dodging tool between the light source and projected image, and then cover the area to be dodged. You'll see that the greater the distance between the paper and the dodging tool, the larger the area that is dodged. Next, *feather*, or move the tool back and forth quickly over the area. Don't just place the dodging tool over the area and hold it there; you'll create a tonal edge that is simply too forced and obvious. Create a number of dodging tools for your work. Have small, medium, and large boards cut into round, oval, and rectangular shapes. You'll find a use for each shape and size. The shapes should be cut precisely to give you more control.

Although there aren't any set rules about dodging, it's usually wise to limit dodging to less than one-quarter of the total exposure time. Any longer and the effect may be too obvious. For example, if total exposure time is 20 seconds, dodge for no more than 5 seconds. If you still can't get detail in the area, you may be working with a lost cause and/or may be working on the wrong contrast paper for that particular negative. Experiment with a number of prints to get the right proportion of dodging to overall printing times. If you blend your light well, you might be able to get away with a higher proportion of dodging to printing time.

Dodging should never be overdone because too much will become obvious and weaken the look of the overall image. Shadow areas are truly darker than the rest of the image, so they shouldn't be weaker in tonal rendition. An "over-dodged" area will be quite apparent and will look pale and muddy. Dodge with a light touch, and be sure that you've done the best you could to get as many of the tones of the negative into the print.

BURNING IN

When you add exposure to select portions of the print over and above the tested printing time, you're burning in. Generally, you burn in to add detail or texture to highlight areas. However, you might also burn in dark areas to get blacker blacks or to obscure shadow areas for a more dramatic representation. A technique called *edge burning* adds a subtle touch of exposure to the sides of a print. This is a way to make the center of the print slightly brighter than the edges. It is also used to correct for extra density buildup that can occur on the edges of a negative during development, and to equalize exposure throughout large areas—such

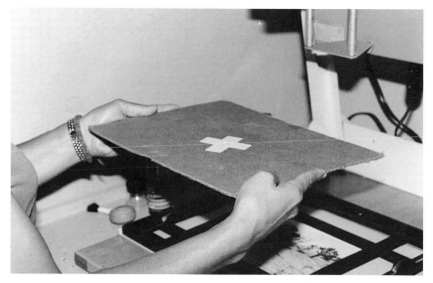

The simple piece of cardboard shown on the left is used for edge-burning prints. Note the cross in the center of the board. Within the cross is a punched-out hole, which can be covered or uncovered for selective burning.

You'll find that your hands are quite versatile tools for burning in and dodging and can form almost any shape necessary. The hands are close to the easel in these pictures simply for the sake of illustration; in practice, your hands can be as close to or as far from the easel as required.

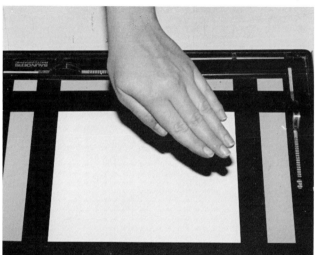

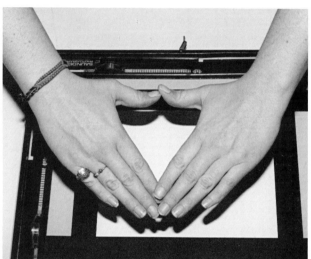

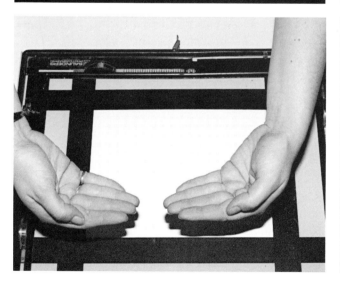

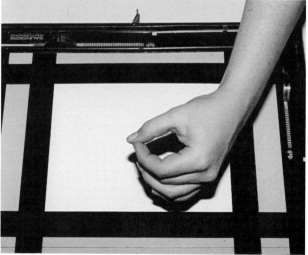

When scene contrast is high and you expose to get details in the shadows, you might have a negative that requires some burning in or dodging. I usually find it easier to expose for the shadow detail and then burn in the highlights, rather than vice versa. If burning becomes complicated, you might find it helpful to diagram your strategy, as shown here. You can often find appropriate burn times from your test-strip print. In the scene on the top of the page on the left, good shadow detail was obtained on a #2 paper with a 6-second exposure time. The "map" for burning was then traced on the work print, shown on the top of the page on the right. I arrived at these times by testing and checking the test-strip print. I based each subsequent burn on the 6-second initial time. For example, 1½ indicates a 9-second additional exposure. Hashmarks indicate an edge burn. The final print shown directly above is the result of quite a bit of testing, but once I go through the steps, making similar prints in the future is easy.

as a sky—of similar tone in such a negative. First, follow the same checks discussed in the dodging section to make sure that the cause of your problem isn't improper paper-contrast selection or too little printing time. If the contrast is too high, you might have good separation in your shadow areas but harsh highlights; conversely, if the printing time is too brief, the blacks will be weak and muddy.

For the most part, you'll find that you'll be burning in to counter the harshness of contrasty scenes, where the brightest tonal areas print with little or no detail, but in which the overall print contrast is just where you want it. Areas needing burning-in treatment may include artificial-light sources in low-light scenes, reflections from metallic objects, or even a sky that is overexposed in relation to the ground.

You can burn in with your hands, with holes cut out in opaque cardboard, with the edge of a board, or with templates. First, if you've ever used your hands to make shadows on a wall, you have an idea of what a versatile tool your hands can be for burning in. Nearly any shape can be created by manipulating your fingers and palms, from straight lines to curving arcs. In addition, you can use both hands to create a funnel of light (see the illustrations on page 89) and can vary the amount of light going through by simulating the aperture on a lens by moving your hands in and out. Burning in by hand takes some practice, but as you gain experience you'll find it to be very valuable.

The most common way printmakers burn in is with a hole cut in a piece of opaque paper or cardboard. Once you determine the area to be burned in, cut a shape in the paper or card that corresponds to the area (the larger the area, the greater the diameter of the hole), place the paper between the light source and the paper, and feather the light onto the area. As you'll see, the farther away you hold the card from the paper surface the greater the area of the projected circle of light. Two tips: First, make sure that the burning in tool is quite a bit larger than the printing paper on which you're working; this ensures that you'll have no unwanted light leaking over the edges of the card onto the outside edges of the printing paper. Second, burn in by moving the tool around to blend the edges of the light to the area rather than just holding the edges of the

card in one spot. As with dodging, creating a seamless look in which tones flow from one area of density to another is critical.

One advantage of working with an opaque card is that you don't have to watch the light hitting the paper on the easel. By holding the burning tool above the easel you can see exactly where the light is playing on the print by looking at the top of the card itself. This increases your control. This close viewing is an invaluable technique because it turns what can be a clumsy experience into a smooth operation.

You can also use a card to burn in edges, corners, or a large horizontal or vertical area of the print, such as skies. Here, you use the same blending or feathering technique to get a flow of tones. Again, make sure that you don't inadvertently burn in areas that have already received enough light.

If you have an odd shape to burn in—one that can't be handled by any other method, such as a city skyline—you can create a template of the area by laying a cardboard or thick paper on the projected print and sketching out the area around the form. You then cut out the shape to be burned in and use it as a burn-in card. As with any card, move it slightly as you work to feather the edges. Keep in mind that you may have to do additional blending with the small cutout burn card to keep the tonal borders from looking false. You can also use this technique for dodging tricky shapes. This technique requires practice to master.

SPLIT-FILTER PRINTING

You can also burn in and dodge to get varying grades of contrast on the same print with VC paper, using what is called the *split-filter printing technique*. This is a way of solving some problems that can't be handled with a graded contrast paper. Consider, for example, that you have a difficult negative, one that has a contrasty sky that calls for a low contrast to bring out detail, as well as a slightly underexposed foreground that would normally call for a #3 contrast grade.

One way to deal with this situation is to boost the overall contrast with a #3 filter, then burn in the sky. This might work well, but too much burning in can result in a harsh-looking print, even though the exposure is correct. With VC papers, you can make the first exposure for the

Split-contrast printing enables you to work with two contrast grades on the same sheet of VC paper. The shot above on the left was made using a #1 filter. The foreground and top of the picture are well exposed, but the center is both too dark and too flat to bring out detail. The print above on the right was made on a #1 paper exposed for the shadows and is also too flat. The picture on the right was also printed for shadow detail, but here the VC paper was exposed through a #3 VC filter. Note the improved contrast. To make the final print, shown on the opposite page, I exposed the foreground and top area through a #1 VC filter and the center area through a #3 filter. This allowed me to control where the print was dense and to boost contrast where it was thin, in the shadows. Split-contrast printing takes practice, but it can certainly get you out of some jams.

foreground with the #3 filter. Then, being careful not to bump the enlarger or to change the focus, substitute a #1 filter. Next, expose the sky with this filter in place, dodging the foreground with your hand or an opaque sheet of paper as you do.

Of course, you'll have to test exposure times on each section of the print as if they were separate images. Don't be too concerned if the #1 filter exposure spills over a bit onto the #3 section. When you're finished, you might also discover that some burning in is required to blend the two contrast areas. Again, this takes some practice, but you'll find that this technique

can solve problems and that it takes full advantage VC paper.

How much burning in should you do? The answer, of course, is to burn in as much as necessary in order to get the tones right. If you're shooting in a very contrasty lighting situation and can't or don't balance exposure accordingly, you might have to burn in as much as two or three times the overall exposure, and even then you may have to go more. But if you always have to burn in anytime you shoot on a bright day, you're probably creating problems. So be sure to check your exposure and/or film-development procedures.

PART FIVE
MAKING BLACK-AND-WHITE PRINTS

To fully understand the printing process, you need to go through a printmaking session from start to finish and to see how printmaking choices are made each step of the way. You'll work with a number of negative types: a normal negative, a flat (low-contrast) negative, and a contrasty negative. You'll also learn how a straight print—one that pulls the most tonal range from the negative at hand—can be made from each of these types. Finally, I discuss printing for effect, such as high- and low-key interpretations. Don't forget that the most important aspect of printmaking is the image itself. Technique without content is impressive, yet wasted. Content without technique can still be meaningful, but the full communication of the vision might suffer.

PRINTING NORMAL NEGATIVES

Most of your negatives will—and should—fall into this category. They are the easiest type to print. A normal negative generally prints well—that is, with a full tonal range—on a #2 contrast-grade paper, or with a #2 filter with VC paper. Keep in mind that some printers use a #3 contrast grade as their "normal" paper when printing with a cold-light head; this is because the diffuse nature of the light tends to lower printing contrast.

After you've set up your developing solutions, turned off the room lights, and turned on the safelights, your next step is to place the negative in the carrier. Then lift the lamp house, and slide the carrier in the negative stage until it locks into place. Close the stage gate, and check for any light leaks. If you see excessive light coming out, your carrier might not be sitting correctly.

Take a sheet of paper the same size and weight as the one you're printing on and place it in the easel. Next, adjust the blades to the desired image size with the borders you want. Then turn on the enlarger focusing light on your timer, and open the enlarging lens to its maximum aperture. Raise or lower the enlarger head as needed, and make sure that the projected image extends slightly over the edge of the easel blades so that you get a clean, sharp edge. Go through the focusing procedure already described. Remember, you make an image larger by raising the head and smaller by lowering it. Eyeball the focus first, and then fine-tune it using your grain focuser. If you see *vignetting*—a falling off of illumination—at the edges of the image, you may have the variable condenser of the enlarger set for the wrong negative size. Check the instruction book, and reset it correctly.

After focusing, close down the lens to f/8 (or to a smaller aperture), check the focus again, and turn off the focusing light. If you're working with VC paper, put your chosen contrast filter in place if you haven't already done so. Next, remove the focusing sheet from the easel, being careful not to nudge the easel. (Most easels have non-slip rubber pads on the bottom to keep them from skidding.) Choose a #2 paper (or a sheet of VC paper if you're working with filters), and slip it into the correct slot in the easel emulsion side up. Set your timer and mask for test-strip printing and follow the procedure outlined on page 83.

Immerse the exposed test print face down into the first solution, the print developer. Make sure that the print is soaked with chemistry by turning it over and back with print tongs or gloved hands. Rock the tray slightly to keep fresh solution in contact with the print; don't just let it sit there. You don't, however, have to jab the print with tongs or continually slosh it around with your tongs or hand. In fact, too much jabbing can damage the delicate print emulsion. This should be just a gentle agitation.

After about 2 minutes for FB papers and about 1 minute for RC papers, move the print over to the stop bath. Don't pick the print up and drop it into the stop; hold it aloft and briefly let the solution drain back into the developing tray. The less solution you carry forward the better. Immerse the print in the stop and agitate as before, keeping it in the bath for about 10 to 15 seconds. Follow the same draining process before using the fixer.

Then after agitating the print in the fixer for about a minute (30 seconds is sufficient in a rapid fixer), move it to a rapidly circulating water bath, and let the print wash for about a minute. Then place it on the back of an unribbed tray, squeegee it off, make sure your printing paper is secure in a light-tight box, and turn on the white light. If this is impossible, bring the tray into another room.

Next, check your test strips to determine the exposure time that provides the best whites, blacks, and middle grays. Make a note of this time. If the test-strip print came up too fast in the developer, either cut down on the duration of the bursts or stop down the lens for the next test. On the other hand, if it doesn't come up or prints too light, you can either open up the lens one stop or increase the lengths of the bursts.

Once you've established your optimum printing time and determined that you needn't switch contrast grades or filters for the best rendition, you can make the work print. Set your timer for the chosen exposure, and make a full print of the image at that time. Then run the print through the chemicals as you did before and inspect it. While a test strip enables you to approximate both the contrast and exposure time, there might be areas of the print not covered by your exposure tests that aren't optimally rendered by that particular exposure. You may have to add or subtract a small amount of exposure time for your best working print. The full print also indicates where you may have to dodge or burn in to add or subtract exposure from certain areas.

A common device used for subtle print enhancement is edge burn. This tends to focus the viewer's attention inward and often gives the image area more "punch." Also, when you develop roll film, such as 35mm or 120 format, there is a chance that more developing activity will occur along the edges of the emulsion because the contact between the film and reel traps the developer. This can result in slight differences in density between the edge area and the rest of the negative; this effect is most noticeable in an area of continuous tone, such as a sky or sidewalk. Edge burning eliminates this problem. To do this, use an opaque cardboard that is larger than the print size. Turn on the enlarger and hold the cardboard between the light source and the print paper; this will project the image onto the board. Move the cardboard back and forth, so that the edge of the image "burns" onto the paper, and then cover it again. Treat each edge this way. An edge burn should be applied for a fraction of the total printing time, at the most 10 to 20 percent. Also, keep in mind that test prints don't have to be fixed and washed as thoroughly as your final prints, because you can discard them.

When a negative has a full tonal range, you shouldn't have much trouble making a rich print on a #2 paper. The negative shown above was printed on a #2 paper for 8 sec. at f/8. In the result on the right, the translation of tones is very good, although some burning in should be applied to the foreground.

Two of the main challenges in printmaking are visualizing how you want a print to look and being able to see the potential in each image. For example, the picture on the right is a straight, unmanipulated print made on a #2 paper. The shot below is the result of some dramatic edge burning, an increase of one contrast grade, and, most important, an idea of how the print should look.

PRINTING FLAT NEGATIVES

A flat negative has little contrast because of the scene's lighting conditions at the time the image was made. It can also have low contrast because of underexposure and/or underdevelopment. In the first situation, you might want to further emphasize the low contrast by choosing a low-contrast paper, or to boost the contrast for visual impact by using a high-contrast paper. For problem negatives that result from faulty development or exposure, you usually have to make a judgment call that sacrifices some tonal information, but improves the look of the print.

When printing low-contrast negatives, use paper-grade contrast to enhance the mood or to emphasize subtle density differences in the negative. This negative was tested on VC papers using #2, #3, and #4 VC filters. The tonal separation became greater as the contrast increased. Strips on the test print were exposed in 1-second bursts. For this print, a #3 filter was used; the exposure time was 5 seconds, with an additional 2-to-3-second burning in of the sky. As such, it represents a good compromise between the softer version of the #2 contrast-grade print and the dramatic contrast differences evident in the #4 contrast-grade print. (Photos: Grace Schaub)

Depending upon the subject—such as a foggy morning—low-contrast negatives printed on a low-contrast paper can be very effective. This combination can add a soft, ethereal look to the final image. While this can maintain the character of the scene, careful testing is needed to get it right. You don't want to print too dark because you might end up with a gray veil over the image. "Low contrast" means a fairly limited range of tones. Your goal is to let all of those tones come through in the print. To add some visual punch, choose a higher-contrast paper, such as a #3 or a #4. Doing this will bring both a deeper black and brighter whites to the image. Of course, exposure time is critical. To see how this works, choose a low-contrast negative from your files and make test-strip prints on a #1 and a #3 or #4 paper. You'll notice how each affects the rendition of the tones. Again, your final choice will depend on what works best for a particular image.

Underexposed and/or underdeveloped negatives can pose a real problem. Of course, any detail not recorded on the negative can never be recovered, but you also must realize that the tonal separation that represents the details is weak. Some printers simply consider such negatives as unusable and eliminate them, but there might be times, such as for a job, when you have to make a print anyway or when the image itself is worthy of printing. The solution is to "boost" the image through the use of a higher-contrast paper.

To learn first-hand how detail and tonality can be improved with these thin negatives, make test-strip prints starting with a #3 paper or a #3 filter with VC paper; switch to a #4 if necessary. Throughout my printing career, I've always been amazed at how much information is contained in a thin negative, but it takes a great deal of testing and fairly critical exposure times to retrieve all of it. The main sacrifice you might have to make with thin negatives is in the shadow detail. Saving the overall image might require you to print the dark grays down to black. However, once you see the results, you'll realize that the sacrifice is usually worth it. Keep this in mind when thinking contrast options. All of this points out the need for good exposure and strict developing controls. If you make a mistake, you'll still be able to get an image, but not necessarily an optimum print.

HIGH-CONTRAST NEGATIVES

High-contrast negatives—those negatives that have both dense highlights and thin shadows—might result from excessive scene contrast, push-processing (in which you intentionally underexpose and overdevelop the film to get more effective speed), and extreme overdevelopment. In order to make a good straight print from these high-contrast negatives, you'll need to balance the tonal rendition by using a low-contrast paper. This choice will enable you to better control the highlights in the negatives without sacrificing the other densities.

With this in mind, make your tests using a #1 or even #0 paper, or the appropriate filters with VC paper. However, you should use #0 paper only in rare cases because it usually prints out with almost no true blacks. Using a #1 grade with a soft-working developer can lower print contrast by half a grade. As with high-contrast papers, exposure is critical. Print too dark, and you will create a print with flat, grayish highlights. Print too light, and your shadows will be muddy. Highlight control on high-contrast negatives might also require some burning in. Of course, you can print a high-contrast scene on a #2 or a higher-contrast paper. And the higher the contrast of the paper, the more the contrast is emphasized in the print.

CONTRAST CONTROL

There are a number of ways to control print contrast when enlarging and processing. The following are some simple guidelines, given in order of most impact:

To **raise** image contrast on prints, you can:

- Choose a higher contrast grade paper

- Use a higher filter number with variable contrast papers

- Use a condenser enlarger (as opposed to a a diffusion or cold light head)

- Develop in a straight developer stock solution (in a hard-working developer)

- Raise the temperature of the developer

- Use developer additives

To **lower** image contrast on prints, you can:

- Choose a lower contrast grade paper

- Use a lower filter number with variable contrast papers

- Use a cold light or diffusion enlarger (as opposed to a condenser head)

- Use a soft-working developer (such as Kodak Selectol Soft)

- Dilute the normal developer more than usual

When you print silhouettes,
contrast choice and exposure
can dramatically change the
foreground/background
relationship. I used a #2 paper for
the picture on the right; the result
is fine except when compared with
the shot on the bottom of the
page, which I made on a #4 paper.
I printed both backgrounds to
about the same density, but the
higher contrast of the #4 paper
produced a deeper black in the
silhouette of the tree. Once I
established the best contrast, I
played with exposure. I printed
the center photograph on the
higher-contrast paper with a longer
exposure time than the bottom
shot. The renditions look as if they
were taken at different times of the
day, and the separation of tones in
the higher-contrast paper keeps the
foreground and background from
dissolving into a dark mass.

SOLUTION TEMPERATURES

Temperature control is very important in black-and-white processing. The most profound effect is in film processing. If you alter the temperature by a few degrees, you'll get quite different results. But temperature control is important in paper processing as well. One of the first areas in which you'll discover the need for careful temperature control is in the mixing of powdered chemicals. For example, if Kodak Dektol (or other similar paper developers) is mixed in water at less than 100° F, the chemicals won't dissolve properly and you'll find white flakes floating in the solution. But if you exceed 115° F, the problem will be solved. Of course, liquid-concentrate chemicals eliminate these problems completely.

The optimum temperature for processing paper is 68° F. Cold print-developing solution (below 60° F) yields very weak blacks in your prints. You might react to this by using a more contrasty paper in an attempt to strengthen blacks, but this will throw off the other tones in the image. Conversely, too hot a developing solution can make blacks come up too quickly; this will yield veiled, gray highlights over the normal developing time. Such forced development robs the paper of its potential beauty. However, hot developer does sometimes come in handy. Suppose you have a print in which there is a great deal of burning in and a number of critical areas in which you simply can't control the highlights. After the print has been in the developer for about a minute, take it out of the solution and place it on the back of an unribbed tray. Squeegee the print and, using a cotton swab, apply developer heated between approximately 90° and 100° F to the areas in which you want more tone. Don't rub the solution in; this can abrade the delicate surface. Just apply the developer locally and very gently. This speeds up development.

Although 68° F is the normal temperature for paper developing, I know some printers who make a practice of working at 80° F to get deep blacks. While this works for them, I recommend relying on proper exposure and contrast-grade selection for your tones, not on hot developer. If you keep the developer within the 65°-to-75° F range, you won't go wrong.

Temperature control can be difficult. Solutions can get hot in warmer climes, and cold during winter. One of the best ways to control solution temperatures is to use a *water jacket* or *water-bath system* in which the containers of mixed chemicals stand in a temperature-monitored tray of water. This can be as elaborate as a thermostatically controlled circulation system, or as simple as a deep dishpan of water to which you add hot or cold water as needed. With either method, be sure to keep your thermometer in the chemical solutions, not in the water jacket.

I periodically check solution temperatures when printing. After I mix powdered developer, the bath is hot, so I put ice in a sealed plastic bag and place it in the solution to bring down the temperature to the optimal working range. If the solutions are cold, I immerse an aquarium heater in order to lower their temperatures as necessary. You can also use hot water in a metal film-developing tank placed right in the tray. If you use heaters, be careful; water and electrical devices, regardless of how water-safe they are, don't mix.

PART SIX

PRINTING FOR EFFECT

Although the majority of your printing might involve making straight prints from negatives, you might want to stretch a bit at times and try a more emotional interpretation of an image. These attempts might break some of the "rules" of conventional printmaking, but you're certainly free to explore other visual effects. This approach took hold for me after years of printing other people's negatives as a commercial printer. After a day of doing my best to squeeze every tone out of sometimes poor negatives, I took out my negatives and did everything I could to make the prints as unconventional as possible. Even though my experiments weren't always successful, I allowed myself the time and space to explore the nuances of shadow and light and to see how new approaches can lead to a fresh way of seeing–and appreciating– photographic prints. Take the time to learn how to make straight prints well, but realize that this isn't the only way to print.

Among the techniques I discuss in this section are printing much lighter or darker than conventional wisdom recommends, dynamic burning in and dodging, and using various filters and other devices to change the character of the light used to create the image.

HIGH-KEY PRINTS

One of the techniques you can use for an emotional interpretation of images is *high-key printing*. This means that the predominant tones in the final print are gray and white, the overall effect is soft and muted, and the contrast is low. The impact of these prints is ethereal and dreamlike; they take us far away from the hard-edged reality usually associated with black-and-white prints.

High-key techniques are especially effective for portraits, still lifes, and selected landscapes. For portraits in which you're trying to convey a romantic sense, in still-life images illuminated by soft window light, in landscapes that evoke nostalgia, a high-key approach will enhance the print. When considering which negatives to use for high-key printing, choose those that have a medium-to-low contrast range. Eliminate those that are stark, with areas of deep blacks; these negatives are better suited for high-contrast printing (see page 112). Rather than accentuate the differences in tones, high-key prints lean toward grays and whites. Deep black tones only take away from the effect.

When photographing with high-key printing in mind, remember that tonal range. If you're shooting a portrait and can control the lighting, just move the subject and/or lights into a low-contrast environment. Some still-life images and landscapes automatically lend themselves to high-key effects: foggy mornings, coffee steaming on a sunlit breakfast table, fields of flowers in the late-afternoon mist. Once you develop an eye for scenes that can be printed in high key, you'll be amazed at the soft, dreamy world opened to you. Some photographers use black-and-white infrared film for this effect, which adds a good deal of grain to the mix.

Another high-key shooting technique is using a diffusion filter. This tones down highlight areas by breaking up the light and can reduce overall contrast. You can buy commercially made diffusion filters, or you can simply smear a very thin layer of petroleum jelly over an old ultraviolet (UV) filter in order to achieve some interesting effects. Some fashion and glamour photographers always keep quite a few of these filters handy.

In the darkroom, the only extra items you'll need for high-key printing are a diffuser and a stock of lower-contrast paper. If you work with VC paper, your #1 and #0 filters will be adequate. While you can print on any paper surface, I prefer matte paper for its overall softer look. Dilute your print developer twice as much as usual. As you work with prints, you might want to dilute the developer even more. Keep the solution temperature at the normal 68° F; any warmer temperature tends to increase contrast. Depending on the negative, you can also use a soft-working developer, such as Kodak Selectol Soft, to lower the print contrast; in addition, both cold-light and diffusion enlargers print with less contrast. However, when combined with the lower grades and a soft-working developer, a condenser enlarger can be used as well.

Although negatives that already have a high-key quality might not require it, you should have a diffusion device handy for printing more normal negatives. You can alter the light with a diffusion filter, a mesh stocking, or even the sleeves in which you store your negatives. As long as each device is transparent and easy to manipulate, it will do the trick. Each one yields a slightly different effect. Some yield more diffusion than others and break up the light rays in a different fashion. Experience will show you which type best matches the negative at hand.

Diffusion materials can be placed right in the light path during the entire print exposure. However, you can also control the amount of diffusion by using a combination of straight and diffused exposure times. Suppose you're printing a portrait with a diffusion filter, such as a fog filter normally used on a camera lens. In this situation, you can expose for about one-half to two-thirds the normal exposure time without the filter and the remainder with the filter in the light path. Testing will show you what percentages yield the desired effect. Keep the diffusion material in motion under the lens, and watch for light spills at the edges.

Once your paper is exposed, place it in the print developer for about half the normal time. For quick-developing RC papers, this is about 30 seconds; for FB papers, this is about 60 seconds. When you like the look, immerse the print in the stop bath and proceed normally. Shortened

When trying to achieve a high-key effect, select appropriate subject matter. First, I printed this image on a #3 grade paper, shown above. The print is satisfactory, but the emotional content of the high-key version on the right works better. Then I printed the image on a #1 paper, and I used a diffusion device (a thin mesh stretched over a frame) during exposure. The diffusion softened the edges and gave a muted, early-morning feeling to the print.

developing time restrains the print contrast. However, if your prints have a mottled look, you've either underexposed your image or underdeveloped the print. Don't substitute weak prints for high-key renditions.

Another trick for heightening the high-key effect even more is giving prints a brief bath in a solution that *bleaches*, or reduces, some of the tones. This is especially useful if prints come up with an overall gray veiling. Because of its lower-than-normal contrast grade, Kodak's Farmer's Reducer, available in packet form, can be used for this purpose. Mix the packets with the potassium ferricyanide (A) and hypo (B) in separate trays, tripling the recommended dilution of ferricyanide to give you more control. Dunk the print in the first tray (the bleach) for a few seconds, and then stop the bleaching action by transferring the print to the hypo bath. Don't try to reduce the print entirely in one cycle. Make it a cumulative process by repeating the steps, with a water bath in between, a number of times. Determining when to stop is a subjective decision. Be sure to always wear gloves and work in a well-ventilated area during this procedure, which can be completed in room light (see page 116 for more on bleaching).

Diffusion is often used with portraiture to lend a romantic look to images. The print shown directly above was made on a #2 paper, which yielded a good straight print. The center print was made on a #1 paper, with a sheet of Mylar used as a diffusion device. The thick plastic was feathered between the lens and the paper during exposure. The exposure time was the same for both prints. However, the diffusion cut down slightly on the amount of exposure the paper received, so the diffused version is also a bit lighter. When the print was made on a #4 paper, which shows the effect of the higher-contrast choice, and diffusion was added, as shown on the right, the model's hair seems to have changed color and the "look" is entirely different. (Photos © Jon Schaub; model: Didi DiCandia)

LOW-KEY PRINTS

Here, images are made darker than you might ordinarily visualize in order to portray a particular mood for, perhaps, a somber landscape. Generally, the instinct of most beginning printers is to make every print bright and contrasty, an approach that usually results in deep blacks and "hot" highlights. But a darker rendition of certain scenes can have just as much graphic appeal. This is simply a matter of having faith in the shadows and not being fearful of losing image information.

Low-key prints are usually most successful when printed on a normal- to low-contrast paper, such as a #2 or a #1. Using a #0 paper or filter with VC paper should be done only when you have a very contrasty negative. Going to a higher grade may cause loss of shadow detail. However, there may be times when form or mood is more important than image content, so don't rule out the higher grades altogether. In general, you want to maintain some tonal separation while printing dark. This can be tricky.

With low-key printing, you don't want to go so dark that the image is just a muddle of dark tones. Work with test strips, and judge the values that longer exposure times yield. You can also simply drop a grade from your normal choice, such as from a #2 to a #1, and increase the exposure by half.

With high-key prints, diffusion filters can sometimes be used to enhance the mood. In a sense, low-key printing is much easier since it requires no special techniques aside from what you see and judge to match the image. For example, if you have a normal negative with some fairly bright highlights, you would choose a low-contrast paper and a lengthy exposure time that prints the highlights as middle gray. This will also make all the other deeper tones even darker, but not as dark as if they had been printed on a normal or high-contrast grade.

Low-key prints rely on richness of tone; you're dealing with black through middle gray, with an occasional sparkling highlight. For that reason, there is no room for weak blacks or mottled grays. As with high-key prints, this effect relies on a subtle application of technique, one that is learned through testing and experimentation.

The print on the left contains all the requirements for an effective black-and-white image: highlights; open, detail-rich shadows; and a good tonal range throughout. However, another approach, such as the one shown below, shifts the time of day and establishes a mood. All that I did to create this was to increase in the print exposure time by 50 percent.

HIGH-CONTRAST PRINTS

These are images of extremes, made up essentially of blacks and whites and few, if any, middle grays. They aim for graphic appeal: bold forms, shapes, and lines rather than subtle detail. Of course, not every negative benefits from this dramatic approach, and it asks you to violate the rules of straight printing, such as seeking texture in the highlights and shadows or a full tonal range in your prints. However, the resulting images are strong, bold interpretations of reality.

The degree of high contrast you can create depends on both the original negative and the paper and chemicals you use. Naturally, a negative that has inherently high contrast will simply make the process easier. However, a normal negative can also be manipulated to yield high-contrast results. The paper choice is in the high-contrast-grade range, either a #4 or a #5, or VC papers with #4 or #5 filters. These contrast grades are ordinarily used to pull detail out of very underexposed and/or underdeveloped, as well as very flat negatives. Here, though, you exploit them to print out very deep blacks and very bright whites from the image. To emphasize the effect, use an undiluted cold-tone stock developer.

You can also increase developer temperature to get richer blacks, but don't go to extremes. A very hot developer (90° F) gives deep blacks but it might also fog, thereby degrading the whites. You can also bleach prints that might have picked up too much texture in the whites. The ferricyanide solution attacks the white and gray densities before the blacks, so you have time to experiment. Another way to produce high-contrast prints is to start with a positive slide and then print onto a high-contrast film (see page 124).

When you have an super-high-contrast negative, you might have to make a choice: to bring it closer to normal tones by using a low-contrast paper, or to keep the high-contrast look by using a normal or even a high-contrast paper. Here, the negative had almost no middle tones. The print I made on a #1 paper, shown above, brings some tone to the snow, but it is a grayness imposed by overexposure of the highlights. I made the shot on the right using a #3 paper, which accentuates the graphic effect. There is no right or wrong decision; just use the print interpretation that matches your feelings about the scene.

EMPHASIZING GRAIN

For many printers, the fabric that holds the black-and-white print together is grain. Others, however, do everything they can to minimize grain; indeed, this seems to be the aim of film manufacturers. Today's 35mm films have very tight grain structures, so photographers can shoot the small format and fool a viewer into thinking that they used a medium-format camera. This might have its purposes, but there is no denying the allure of grain and its intimate involvement with the feel of a black-and-white image.

The starting point for emphasizing grain is film speed. Generally, the faster the film, the larger the grain. Special-purpose films, such as Kodak Recording film and infrared black-and-white film, are often used for their grainy results. You can also boost grain in conventional film by either combining underexposure with overdevelopment, increasing the temperature of film-processing solutions, or processing the film in very active developers. For example, Kodak Tri-X developed in Dektol, the print developer, for 1½ minutes yields developed in a very dense, grainy negative.

When you print, you can further emphasize grain by enlarging to a high magnification and severely cropping the image. If your enlarger can't go high enough to suit the desired effect, you can also use a shorter lens than normal to obtain a bigger image size at more reasonable enlarger-head heights. This may cause vignetting at the edges of the image, but that doesn't matter if your primary subject occupies only a small portion of the frame. Mounting a 28mm lens on your lensboard can truly do wonders; these lenses are available in many used-camera stores and were once sold as interchangeable lenses for cine cameras.

Another way to boost the appearance of grain is to print on a contrast grade that's higher than normal. The higher the contrast, the more the contrast within the salt-and-pepper pattern of the grain. Of course, this means more image contrast. As discussed, a condenser enlarger head produces a slightly more contrasty image and increases the appearance of grain.

TONING

Many types of toners exist. Some stain the entire print with color; others are used for coloration and to plate or convert the silver in the print to a more stable form. A wide variety of toners come in commercially available powdered and liquid forms; formulas for more exotic varieties can be obtained through technical books. I tend to limit my toning to those available commercially. Check the technical books if you have an interest in mixing your own toners.

Commercial and noncommercial toners enable you to make the relatively neutral color of a silver-based image blue, brown, sepia, red, and various shades in between. Each color, whether it is the golden/brown sepia for a nostalgic portrait or a deep blue for landscapes of a snowy field, can lend a different feeling to a picture. Toners can be used in different strengths to get more or less intensity of color in an image, and individual papers react quite differently to various toning baths. Aside from aesthetic considerations, most toners increase the lifespan of prints by either plating the silver or combining with the silver in order to form another metallic compound, one that better withstands the test of time.

You can change the color of prints by coloring them with dyes. This stain affects the highlights and the silver-rich areas of the print equally, and makes the print look as if a colored gel has been placed over the image. This technique works well for quick display or illustrative prints, and you can easily add different colors to various parts of the image. However, these dyes don't convert the silver.

There are two main types of converting toners: bleach-and-redevelop toners and single-bath toners. Bleach-and-redevelop toners, such as Agfa Viradon (a toner that can be used for bleach-redevelop or single-bath systems) and Kodak Sepia toner, work in a two-step process. First, you bleach the silver with a solution of potassium ferricyanide (Part A of the Kodak Sepia toner package) and then replace it with a sodium sulfide or thiourea solution (Part B). Sepia toning is excellent for bucolic, nostalgic images: landscapes, portraits, and copy prints of old pictures. It closely matches the look of prints from days long gone. However, the sepia effect isn't subtle, and the print color can overwhelm the image. When you bleach the print, you must wait until the image itself has nearly disappeared from the paper, then you immerse the print in the second tray and the picture reappears, with a warm brown color.

Single-bath toners, such as Kodak Rapid Selenium, Agfa Viradon, Kodak Brown, Kodak Polytoner, and Berg Brilliant Blue and Copper toners, afford you more control over the degree of print color than sepia toner does. By using various dilutions and immersing the print in the toner for different lengths of time, you can add just a touch or completely change the color of the image. For example, I use Kodak Rapid Selenium toner as a regular part of my FB printing. If I want to impart a reddish-brown tone to the image, I mix the toner 1:3 and leave the print in the bath from 5 to 7 minutes. However, if I want to keep the print color essentially unchanged, I mix it 1:36 and leave it in the bath for about 3 minutes. This converts the silver without producing any noticeable color shift. Many darkroom workers use Kodak Rapid Selenium toner mixed 1:12. This dilution does the conversion and "clears" the whites a bit—all without causing any noticeable color shift.

Because you're changing the color of the image, the print density may appear to lighten. When I have sepia toning in mind, I tend to make prints about 10 to 20 percent darker than normal. Other toners reduce densities less, although they may bleach slightly and open up shadow areas to reveal more detail.

As discussed earlier, dilution equals control. With most toners, the more you dilute the stock solution with water, the slower the toning process. Some toners, such as Kodak Polytoner, actually yield different colors according to dilution. The more dilute the stock, the warmer brown the print color. Refer to the toner's packaged directions for details.

Each paper differs in its response to toning baths. Testing reveals sometimes subtle, sometimes great differences among them. For example, Agfa Portriga, a warm-tone paper, picks up a warmer, more golden-brown tone in sepia toner than a cold- or neutral-tone paper, such as Agfa Brovira, does; it can tone more to a cold magenta-brown color. The beauty of some "art" papers is only truly revealed with toning; you should test all the toners with these papers to see how they behave.

While toning itself is a fairly simple procedure that takes place solely in white light—mix the toner, insert the print, and watch what happens—you should check for certain things when you initially process the print you intend to tone. First, you should keep in mind that the use of a nonhardening fixer makes it more difficult for the toner to penetrate and might even cause stains. Once your prints are properly fixed, you must wash them thoroughly because too much residue causes stains during toning. Remember, fixer residue is the chief culprit in causing stains in toned prints, so be sure to take special care at this point.

Some toners are irritants; others are downright poisonous. Wear gloves, aprons, and even goggles, and always work in a well-ventilated area. While your first reaction to the fumes might be adverse, you may shrug it off once you get used to the smell. Don't let this fool you; get some air moving every time you tone.

Toning can be done at any time after the print is made—weeks, months, or even years later. For that reason, I tend to batch my prints and tone all at once, rather than to do a few prints at a time. If you're toning prints that have already dried, soak them thoroughly in water before you begin. As with all techniques, experimentation and recording your observations will help you predict future results.

TONING COMBINATIONS

Papers and toners can be combined to achieve different color and color-intensity effects in your prints. This chart shows a sampling of combinations, as well as some variables that are introduced when different paper developers are used. All the products shown here are from Eastman Kodak; papers and toners made by other manufacturers can also be mixed and matched.

Paper	Developer	Toner	Color	Color Effect
Elite	Dektol	Selenium 1:12	Slight	Purplish brown
Elite	Dektol	Sepia	Full	Cool brown
Panalure	Selectol	Brown	Full	Warm brown
Panalure	Selectol	PolyTone 1:50	Full	Chocolate brown
Panalure	Selectol	Sepia	Full	Yellowish sepia
Polycontrast III	Dektol	Brown	Full	Reddish brown
Polycontrast III	Dektol	Sepia	Full	Cool brown

CHEMICAL REDUCTION: BLEACHING

No matter how carefully you expose your prints, there is always room for improvement. For example, you might have a portrait with skin tones perfectly balanced, but the eye area might be somewhat dull and lifeless. Dodging could be the answer; however, if the whites of the eyes are only a tiny portion of the print, you might find it quite difficult to get it right without dodging adjacent areas. You also may try going to a higher contrast grade paper to enliven the eyes, but the skin tones will be less pleasing. In another print of a cityscape at night, you may have solved the problem of the deep-shadow detail of the buildings by reducing contrast, but the streetlights may be a dull gray; here again, dodging or using a higher-contrast paper may cause more trouble than assistance.

The answer to this and other such difficulties is selective chemical reduction of certain densities, a technique commonly referred to as bleaching. Used carefully, bleaching can be a subtle technique that leaves no trace of any manipulation; overdoing it, though, can be quite a distraction. For instance, too much bleaching in the eyes can make subjects look like vampires; too much in a night scene can impart a harsh, false look to the image.

Bleaching is done with two chemicals: fixer and potassium ferricyanide. You can buy potassium ferricyanide in large, 1-pound bottles or, if you want to give it a try, use Part A of the two-part package of Kodak Farmer's Reducer. This chemical comes in crystalline form; check its freshness by making sure that it is a bright orange-red; a dull or brownish red means that the chemical has oxidized, which reduces its effectiveness. When you mix and work with this chemical, which you can do in ordinary household light, always use gloves and work in a very well-ventilated area.

Mix a small quantity of the red crystals in a glass container of water, and stir until all the crystals are dissolved. Just a pinch of crystals in a shotglass is fine. Once the liquid turns a very light yellow, it is done. Too deep a yellow—the color of the first step of sepia toning—means that the solution is too concentrated and will work too fast for proper bleaching control.

Some instruction books call for a stronger dilution, but remember, dilution equals control.

The second solution is using plain fixer (without hardener). Mix it as you normally would. You'll be using more of this solution than the potassium-ferricyanide solution, so don't be afraid of mixing too much. Gather cotton swabs; cotton balls; a fine brush (A #000 or #0000 artist's brush); a squeegee; a plastic water-bath tray; and an empty, unribbed tray (or plate glass or any other flat surface). If your brush has a metal collar, coat it with a hard lacquer, such as fingernail polish, to prevent the potassium ferricyanide from causing it to corrode. Mark the brush so that you don't use it for anything else.

You can do this right after your normal processing steps, or you can re-soak prints later to work on them. Take the wet print from the water tray, and let it drip dry. Next, place it on the back of the unribbed tray, and squeegee off the excess water. Dip your cotton swab or fine brush into the red bleach solution, tap it or let it drip until it is fairly dry, and then apply it to the area to be reduced. Be sure to wear rubber gloves when bleaching.

Suppose, for example, that you're working on an eye and want to lighten the whites. Move the applicator over the areas until all of them are covered; in a few seconds, you might begin to see the bleach work, but don't let it go all the way to the intended density. Instead, take a cotton ball soaked in hypo and apply it to the areas. This serves both to catalyze and to stop the bleaching action. Keep in mind that the bleach continues to work for a while, so stop before you reach the desired effect.

After you've done this once, study the tone. If it is where you want it to be, dip the print briefly in a tray of fixer to make sure that you've completely neutralized the bleach, and then wash the print normally. If you still want to go lighter, repeat the procedure. This should be a gradual process, and control is quite important. Once the tones are gone, they're gone; that is why overdilution is so critical.

It is also important to squeegee the print dry between applications. Any water runs filled with bleach will affect undesired areas. Be sure to watch for pockets of water that can become pools of density-reducing bleach. Also, don't rub the reducing or fixing solution into the print because any rubbing can abrade the print surface. If you are patient and work slowly, bleaching can give your print touches of brilliance. You can also use bleaching for overall print reduction to save a print that has been printed too dark. This technique works on all the tones at once, but acts upon the highlight areas much more quickly than it does on the denser shadow areas and blacks. However, this remedial touch isn't a substitute for making proper exposure and contrast choices.

If a print comes out too flat, you might be able to save it with a quick, overall bleaching. This can bring snap to dull highlights and open up some shadow detail. Bleaching works first on the highlights and then on the denser areas in the print. I made the photograph above on a #2 paper and overexposed, so that the highlights went gray. A quick run through a bleaching solution opened up the print, as shown on the right. While bleaching shouldn't be an excuse for poor printing technique, it can come in handy.

PRINT DRYING

When you buy photographic paper, it is flat—just the way it is when it comes out of the final wash. The problem with FB papers occurs during drying, when the print curls slowly. This happens because the emulsion and paper base dry at different rates and/or the emulsion shrinks a bit during the dry-down. While prints can be dry-mounted to straighten them out, too much of a twist may result in emulsion cracking if it is mishandled in any way. That is why it is essential to dry prints according to prescribed methods.

RC papers don't pose this problem because they're made to dry flat. To dry these papers, simply take the print out of the final wash, squeegee it off, and lay it flat on racks or hang it on a line. FB papers, on the other hand, can be dried in a number of ways. Ask 12 printers how they dry their prints, and you might get 10 different answers. One method is to use fiberglass screens stretched and stapled over frames. These are available commercially from a number of sources, or you can build them yourself. Here, you simply squeegee your prints several times, then place them face down on the screen surface and allow them to air dry. They will curl slightly, but placing them face down helps keep this under control; they curl toward the emulsion side of the paper. Once dry, a brief stint in a dry-mount press (about 15 seconds at 200° F) between pre-dried smooth boards will completely flatten them. If you don't own a dry-mount press, check your local photo store or camera club in order to obtain one.

You can also place a second screen on top of the one on which your prints are drying. The frames will keep the screens separate, while the top screen minimizes curl. You'll still have to use a heated press to eliminate the slight curl, but some printers find that placing prints under a weight, such as a heavy plate glass, is effective.

Another method is to use blotting paper made specifically for photographic use (blotters made for non-photographic use might contain materials that can harm prints and should be avoided). Blotters come in book, roll, or loose-sheet form. I prefer loose sheets because they can be easily dried individually. When using blotters, you must first remove as much water from the print as possible. Lift the print from the wash and let it drain well. Then squeegee off both the front and back several times. Check that the squeegee has no dings or burrs in it; the paper is very delicate at this point. Use light pressure and repeated runs, rather than trying to get all the water out with one heavy pass.

Next, lift the paper gently from the edge and place it face down on a sheet of clean blotter paper. If the blotter shows signs of stain or discoloration—usually caused by fixer contamination—throw it away. These stains will attach themselves to the wet paper. Once a blotter sheet is filled with a single layer of prints, place another blotter on top and repeat until you have a stack of blotters. Then reverse the whole stack. This blotter should be quite wet now.

The next step is to remove the prints from the top blotter and place them in a fresh set of blotters. Hang the blotters you've used on a line to dry. Continue down through the pile and repeat the cycle of blotter, prints, blotter, prints. Wait about 30 minutes, and repeat the whole cycle. This time, however, place two blotters between each layer of prints. Wait an hour and repeat the process, this time placing three blotters between each print layer. Now place a wide, flat weight, such as the plate glass, on top of the whole stack. Your prints should come out of this pile dry and flat in a few hours.

If you want a high-gloss finish on FB prints, you'll have to use a ferrotype plate dryer. The ferrotype dryer is usually based on a heat-drying system. Here, make sure that the drum or platen is heated to at least 180° F before you run your prints through. To help ensure a smooth gloss, soak prints in a very mild solution of a wetting agent (just a few drops to the gallon), such as Kodak Photo-Flo, before putting them through this process. Place the prints emulsion side down against the ferrotype plate.

The highly polished metal surface of the ferrotype plate must be scratch-free. Any mark on the surface will probably emboss the surface of the print. And the blotter or cloth used as a backing must be clean and free of hypo stains. If you use a ferrotype dryer in a school environment or communal darkroom, insist that the blotter be clean. If it isn't, your efforts will be wasted. Never put RC prints through a ferrotype-heat dryer; the plastic print surface will melt and/or stick to the metal plate.

PRINT SPOTTING

Unless you work in a dust-free environment, vacuum your negatives before you print, and pass through the equivalent of a static-free airlock when entering your darkroom, you're going to have some spots on your prints. These spots are formed by dust, either on the negative itself or on some part of the light path in the enlarger. These flecks, large or small, manifest themselves as white blemishes, and if they're not removed, will greatly detract from the enjoyment of the print. When you enlarge a negative, you enlarge the dust, so even a small piece of dirt is obvious.

When you print, clean your negatives with a burst of compressed air or wipe them with a camel's-hair or antistatic brush; if dirt is embedded in the emulsion—usually a result of drying negatives in a dusty environment—rewash the negative to remove it. Also, check your condensers, which are magnets for dust, and keep your lens clean. Even if dust doesn't print as obvious specks, a dirty lens can hurt print sharpness. As discussed earlier, a cold-light head might eliminate some need for spotting. However, even with the greatest care, you'll have to deal with some spotting when you print.

Print spotting entails blending the white specks on the print surface with the tonal areas immediately surrounding them, thereby creating the illusion that they never existed. This blending is accomplished by applying dyes that match the surrounding color and tone.

MATERIALS NEEDED

To apply the dyes, you'll need a spotting brush, which is available in photo- and art-supply stores. Choose a brush coded #000 through #00000; the finer the brush, the higher the number of zeroes. Since spotting is a gradual process, the finer the brush, the more the control you have in the process. Get one for ammonia, and one for spotting.

Spotting dyes are made especially to match the color of photographic papers and to soak into the emulsion. You match the color by using these dyes straight or by combining them to obtain subtle nuances. A number of companies sell these dyes. I have used Spotone brand for years. This brand comes in half-ounce bottles.

The company offers a #0, for olive-black tones; a #1, for cold tones; a #2, for selenium-toned prints; a #3, for neutral tones; a #B, for brown-toned prints; and a #S, for sepia-toned prints. The instructions tell you how many drops of each dye it takes to make a blend that matches the image tone of virtually all available black-and-white papers. Aside from these dyes, you'll need a palette for blending colors, a shotglass of water, a sponge or paper towel, some wetting agent, and a small bottle of highly dilute ammonia.

THE STEP-BY-STEP PROCEDURE

First, blend a number of spotting colors in order to get different variations of the basics. I use a circular watercolor palette with nine receptacles, into which I first place the basic colors, then fill in the rest with combinations. For example, I'll put equal parts of #1 and #3, or #3 with #0, and so forth. I label each receptacle and allow the dyes to dry completely.

When I begin to spot, I use a sheet of the same photographic paper used for my print (a test print or work print will do) for color testing. Although I have found that certain combinations match certain papers—such as straight #3 for Agfa Brovira printed in Dektol; or #3, #0, and #2 combined for Agfa Portriga in Selectol; the colors in each paper vary according to print developer, temperature, and the age of the paper, among other elements. There are just too many variables at play to give set rules for matching ink to paper type; you'll simply have to have a number of combinations available to cover the bases. Nothing shows that a print has been spotted like a mismatched color, so take some time with this step.

To test color—and to actually spot later—wet the tip of the brush on a slightly moist sponge and put the brush into the dry dye. Make a few strokes on the back of an old print in order to dry the brush, then lay strokes on the side of the test print to see how well the color matches. Once you have a close match, you can go to your main print.

Rather than work in broad strokes, you must stipple the spot with the tip of the brush, working in a small area and building up the density of color as you go. Gradually extend the spotting into a larger area. For example, when working on a hairline, don't use a single, long sweep. A line is a series of connected dots, so that is how you should attack it when spotting. Work with the grain if it is visible. Keep the brush nearly vertical so that you use only the tip, and rest your hand on a clean cover sheet to prevent getting marks on the print. Use a light touch—the key to spotting is making dabs.

As you work, the brush will discharge ink so the color and density you're laying down will lose intensity. So either reload with dye or move on to lighter tones, such as the grays and near-whites. Always test shade and intensity on your work print before you switch to lighter areas. Spotting a light area dark shows up even more than no spotting at all.

Mistakes can happen when you're spotting. A brush can slip, or you can use too much or too dark ink. Luckily, these mistakes can be corrected easily. This is where the ammonia comes in. Mix eight drops of household (non-sudsy) ammonia in 4 ounces of water, and then dab the solution on the spot that is too

dark. Use a separate brush for the ammonia, and a napkin to blot the brush tip before application, as too wet a wash can damage the print emulsion. In a sense, you're lifting the spot from the paper, not wiping it away. Make sure that the print is completely dry before re-spotting. At times, you might be able to use this ammonia wash in order to reduce a too-dark spot to just the right density. If you ruin an area on RC paper, soak the whole sheet in a mild wetting-agent solution, dry it, and begin again.

Keep in mind that spotting involves building density. In fact, it is best to spot to slightly less density than required. You might see every nuance up close and get quite particular about matching density, but having a close match that's slightly lighter than the surrounding tones is fine. Admittedly, spotting can be a tedious procedure. This is why keeping your darkroom clean and getting dust off the negative before you print is so critical.

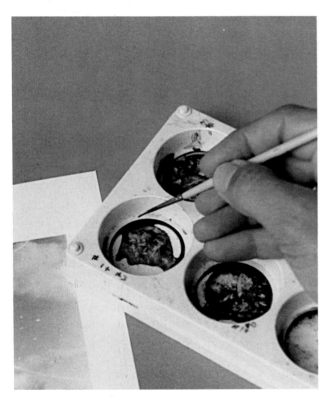

I blend spotting colors in a watercolor palette and allow them to dry; then I work with a slightly moistened brush tip to lift the colors from the dry well. Although some Spotone colors match prints perfectly, I find that various blends, such as 1 + 3 and 0 + 1, work well for the many print colors caused by various paper/developer combinations.

When spotting, use a light touch and work your way around the print from dark to light spotting tasks. Try to spot so that your work is unnoticeable; spot to a tone slightly lighter than the one that surrounds the blemish. Practice and patience are required to master spotting technique.

PROTECTING YOUR PRINTS

Photographs are fragile, subject to attack from a wide range of forces. For a long time, little was understood about what could adversely affect pictures. Now there are volumes of literature on the subject, with more research being conducted every day. Of all photographic materials, black-and-white is right next to those with the potential for the longest lifespan—provided that the printmaker follows certain processing and storage rules. As mentioned, these include processing for permanence, thorough washing and removal of fixer, and a conversion of the silver in the print to a more stable compound through toning. However, all this effort can be futile if you don't take care of your prints after the processing run is long completed. Temperature, humidity, storage, mounting boards, adhesives, the amount of sunlight that falls on prints, and the type of gases in our environment all have an effect on print stability. If you ignore these forces, your prints might stain and fade.

Museums are quite careful about print storage, and they monitor temperature and humidity in their storage areas and galleries. Although most people can't afford these expensive controls, you can still protect your images from heat and humidity. In fact, storage at room temperature (60° to 70° F) is acceptable because temperatures don't fluctuate too much in home storage spaces. Wide fluctuations, such as those in an attic in temperate zones, can cause a cycle of change to speed up. The general rule is: The cooler the better, with as consistent a temperature as possible.

High humidity can also have an impact on images, and the combination of high heat and humidity can be quite destructive. But too little humidity can also cause problems, particularly brittleness. A relative humidity of 40 percent has been found to be optimal. So if your storage area's humidity is far below (10 percent) that, you should consider a humidifier; if the humidity is far above (95 percent) that, you might want to get a dehumidifier.

Too much light on a print can cause fading. Keep displayed prints away from direct sunlight, and/or use a UV-protected glass or plexiglas, available at frame shops. In fact, the best archival storage for black-and-white prints is no light at all. If you frame prints, never place a print directly against the glass; a window matte prevents sticking due to condensation and evaporation.

Proper storage involves choosing appropriate mounting and boxing materials and keeping prints away from damaging gases in the environment. Prints not placed in acid-free boards can be harmed. The prints may be as pure as the driven snow, but the contaminants that leak out of poor-quality wood-pulp board can attack the paper itself. Don't store prints in cheap cardboard containers put together with ordinary adhesives. The adhesives can break down and stain prints, and ordinary cardboard can emit gases that attack the silver. Although they might be more expensive, 100 percent rag, acid-free boards, boxes, and tape—which are used to adhere prints to mattes and backing boards—are worth the price. If you store prints in drawers, choose baked enamel metal rather than wood or cardboard. Again, gases from the latter can cause print deterioration. Fungus can also cause a serious problem with prints. Some varieties feast on the gelatin in photographic emulsions. Believe it or not, bugs also tend to favor prints, and I've even seen cats lick the surface of prints for salt left on because of improper washing. The fungus problem can be eliminated with humidity control; the other problems can be stopped by careful adherence to safe storage practices.

Atmospheric fumes can also be a problem, particularly with the air pollution in many urban centers. Silver can tarnish from many of these pollutants, but following good processing practices can go a long way to safeguard images and negatives. Hydrogen-peroxide fumes, for example, can be insidious. I once made a series of 20 x 24 prints for a beauty salon. A month after the prints were hung, the salon's proprietor stormed back into my lab with what had become faded, purple-stained images. The fumes from the hair-coloring station had ruined them.

How long should your prints last? With proper storage and processing, they'll outlive all of us. Expose them to deteriorating conditions, and you can watch them fade. I've learned from experience that these protective measures should be taken seriously and adhered to.

THE SABATTIER EFFECT

Like many interesting discoveries, the *Sabattier Effect*, also commonly called *solarization,* was a result of a happy accident. This was the fogging of photographic plates with light during development by a Frenchman named, not surprisingly, Sabatier. (Somehow his name and the effect gained another "t" through the years.) This effect can be used with films and/or paper. With film, you can make multiple identical copies of the same solarized image. With paper you have a one-of-a-kind image because results are unpredictable.

When you expose paper to white light during development, you actually reverse some of the image's tones from positive to negative. Whites can turn gray, and low-density lines can form at tonal borders. The result is often a surreal effect that can produce some true graphic play. The impact on the print is most noticeable in those areas that received the least initial exposure, white and grays. But in contrast to the rest of the print the changes can be fascinating. However, there are variables you can control.

Expose your print slightly less than normal, then immerse it in a fairly weak dilution of developer, 1:4 rather than the usual 1:2, and develop the print for about one-half to three-quarters the normal time—about 60 to 90 seconds. Take the print out of the developer, squeegee it off, and place it on the back of an unribbed tray. Hold the tray about 4 feet from a 15-watt bulb and then turn the bulb on and off quickly. This will almost seem as if the light is flickering on and off. (You can do the re-exposure step with the print in the developer, but I've always gotten more consistent quality by removing it first.) Then return the print to the developer, and let it develop completely.

You might notice that the whites have turned too gray or that the print has become totally fogged with light. This might indicate that the white light was on too long, the print was too close to the light, or the initial developing was too short. Try again, varying any or all of these steps. However, don't pull the print from the developer if it comes up too quickly and dark; this will result in weak blacks and a poor image overall. Just throw it away and start again.

If the print is close to what you like but the whites are too dark, you can lighten them by immersing the entire print in a tray of reducing solution. Mix some potassium ferricyanide and water so that the color of the solution is light yellow, soak the print for about 30 seconds, and then bring it into a tray of fixer. This might clear the grays and whites sufficiently to give you a clean, crisp image because the reducing solution works on highlights and middle grays before it attacks the blacks.

The Sabattier Effect is often unpredictable, but it can be very powerful when it comes out right. Experimentation and practice will show you the way to go.

The Sabattier effect is a fun, experimental technique. Although you can solarize film (and get many prints from one solarized negative), I prefer to work only on paper because the randomness is what attracts me in the first place. The picture on the left shows a straight print of a child during Mardi Gras in New Orleans. The shot below is the solarized version.

NEGATIVE PRINTS

Here, the tones of the positive image are reversed back to negative. The easiest way to make such an image is to make a print from a positive image, such as a color or black-and-white slide. If you want to make a negative print from a negative you first have to contact or enlarge the original onto a sheet of copy film, and then print normally.

Although some fascinating images can be created this way, you can take another step to expand the possibilities even further by making a positive from the negative print itself. This allows you to retouch it in a way that can add texture or add and subtract hand-drawn forms to the image. For best results, I suggest using a lightweight matte-surface enlarging paper; it means shorter exposure times and more tooth for retouching. First make the negative print, then use a soft lead pencil to retouch and add density to select areas. Whatever you pencil in will hold back the light during exposure, so it will print lighter or white. You then contact print the retouched print onto a regular sheet of enlarging paper, and check the results.

Take some care while retouching, as any marks you leave will be etched into place. Experiment as you go along, and try your hand at adding stipple, texture, and light and heavy touches. The graphic play available is limitless. You can also add to the effect by toning and handcoloring the final print.

This stark, graphic image was made by enlarging a 35mm color slide (positive) directly onto a sheet of #5 Agfa Brovira paper. Through the use of a paper with such a high-contrast grade, many of the middle gray tones were eliminated. Although this doesn't work with many images, this scene, originally of rocks on a beach, lent itself to abstraction. A positive of this image can be made by contact printing the negative print itself onto another sheet of printing paper.

SUPER-HIGH-CONTRAST PRINTS

As discussed earlier, you can make high-contrast images from conventional negatives (see page 124) by using high-contrast grade paper, undiluted developer, and a condenser-enlarger head. But extreme high-contrast images—that is, just black and white—can be obtained by adding another step. This is creating a super-high-contrast negative from an original negative or slide, and then enlarging or contacting it onto high-contrast paper.

To create a high-contrast negative, you'll need a film such as Kodak Kodalith Ortho or Kodalith Pan film; these are available in pro shops and graphic-arts supply stores. The main difference between the two is that the Ortho film is "blind" to red light, so you can watch it develop out in a tray just like paper. Kodalith Pan film should be developed in total darkness; it is somewhat blind to a dark green light, but this may be too dim for you to inspect. Although I've developed both of these films in Dektol, the best results for high contrast are obtained with Kodak Kodalith developer, an A and B mix that you combine when you're ready to work. Naturally, the density you record on these negative films depends on exposure. A strong exposure will give denser images, but one with less density can also give unusual effects. Test strips will reveal the differences.

You can make a negative or a positive image with this film. Expose a negative on to it, and you get a positive; expose a positive, such as a color or black-and-white slide, and you'll get a negative image. You can also contact the positive image to another sheet of film and process normally, and you'll get another negative. You can continue this procedure ad infinitum to achieve different effects.

As with negative prints, you can change the image any way you wish by opaquing the negative with India ink or a special opaquing liquid, available in the same shop in which you picked up the film. Always work on the emulsion side of the film when opaquing because it has the best "tooth," or surface, to hold the application. This liquid or ink can also be used to correct white spots in the negative caused by dust; in a sense, you spot the negative as you do a print. Working clean eliminates imperfections.

Once you have the negative, you can proceed normally for the high-contrast effect, using a #5 paper or filter with VC paper and straight, undiluted developer. You can also reduce the print in a potassium ferricyanide bath to bleach out any gray tones that might have developed. Naturally, the image will determine your success with this effect. Choose those with bold lines and forms, or that lend themselves to a more graphic representation. You can also tone or handcolor these images later for even more play.

Originally shot on color-slide film, this graphic image was given heightened contrast. First, a negative was made on high-contrast film, then enlarged normally on a high-contrast paper. To ensure that the image would stay sharp when it was converted to a negative, the slide was removed from its mount and contact printed onto the film. When using this or any other special-effects technique, let the subject matter of the image be your guide. (Photo © Grace Schaub)

DIFFUSION PRINTING AND VIGNETTING

We've already discussed diffusion in the context of high key printing, but it can be used in conventional printmaking as well. Using the same tools we add to the light path—diffusion filters, glass with petroleum jelly, and so forth, you can soften edges, break up highlights or make cosmetic changes to a subject's face. When working with glass diffusion you can also selectively diffuse parts of the image and eliminate distracting elements or add an ethereal, dreamlike touch to any scene.

Vignetting is a technique used by portraitists to eliminate distracting elements or to concentrate a viewer's attention on the main subject alone. You can easily vignette a scene by cutting out an oval or any other shape in a piece of cardboard and printing through it onto the paper. Keep the oval mask moving during exposure to blend the edges of the cut. You can also add some density to the dodged area by first making your initial exposure with the oval mask, then removing the negative from the carrier and, with a dodging tool over the center of the image burning in the edges of the frame. This takes away some starkness that may be evident when printing with the vignetter alone.

This head shot was originally a three-quarter-length pose. The image was cropped through the use of a cardboard with an oval mask cutout, which allowed only a portion of it to be exposed on the printing paper. To add to the diffusion effect, a sheet of mylar was held beneath the cutout during exposure. Also, the cardboard was feathered during exposure in order to avoid any definite tonal borders on the print. (Photo © Grace Schaub)

TRANSFORMING COLOR INTO BLACK-AND-WHITE

Although the best quality comes from printing from black-and-white negatives, photography is an interchangeable medium that enables you to make high-quality black-and-white prints from color materials as well. There may be times when you have only color in your camera, and decide later that a black-and-white rendition may work as well.

For the best results from color-negative film, use panchromatic paper, such as Kodak Panalure. This type of paper is sensitive to all wavelengths of light. However, because the paper is sensitive to all colors of light, you can't work in normal safelight illumination; the paper will fog if you do. The best way to avoid fogging is to make your test-strip print and then develop it in darkness. You might be tempted to cheat and turn on the safelight and look at a print very near the end of the developing step, but you should wait until the print is safely in the fixer first. Check your test strips as you would normally, and then make a final print, again turning off the safelights when you do.

To make a black-and-white print from a color slide, you'll have to make an internegative on black-and-white film, and then make a print from it. However, slides tend to be quite a bit more contrasty than negative films, and using conventional films might cause a problem with some scenes. One of the best films to use for this internegative is a professional copy film. These films have a double emulsion that gives good highlight separation. If you use a conventional film, decrease development by about 20 percent or use a low-contrast negative developer to control contrast. Ilford XP-1 is a chromogenic black-and-white film that is particularly good for internegative stock.

You can make an internegative using the enlarger to project the slide onto the sheet film, or you can contact print the transparency film right onto the copy film (remove it from the mount for better sharpness). You can also use a slide-duping machine for this. Many of these have contrast and color-filtration controls.

As discussed, the negative is the foundation of the print. For certain special effects, you can begin with an unconventional film in the camera, and then use your many printing techniques to explore the effects even further. There are high-contrast films for graphic-arts applications, surveillance films that yield super-high grain, and "instant" films from Polaroid for positive black-and-white slides in both high- and normal-contrast formulations.

Whatever effects you choose, keep in mind that they should serve the image. That's the point of all the techniques in this book. Don't make printing an end in itself. It is a means of communicating the feelings that motivated you to take the picture in the first place.

HANDCOLORING

This has been a part of photographic tradition since the earliest days of the medium. At first, it was used as a way to bring color to a monochrome medium. Today, handcoloring has developed a new following among art and advertising image makers all over the world. You can add color to entire prints and make them as "real" or surreal as you desire. You can also just add a dash of color to accent a particular object or mood in the scene. When handcoloring, choose a matte-surface paper, which provides the best "tooth" to grab and hold the colors. For portraits, work with a warm-tone paper, or tone a cold-tone paper with sepia or brown toner. This color "wash" makes skin tones appear more natural and eliminates any clash between the paper color and the colors you add.

One of the best mediums for handcoloring is Marshall Photo Oils. These are transparent colors made especially for photographic prints. You can, however, also use colored pencils, pastels, watercolors, or acrylic oils. Some artists use the print as a type of coloring book on which they apply any number of mediums. When using photo oils work lightly, and then blend and layer colors as you go along. With the right brushes, cotton swabs, and cotton balls for larger areas of color, you can work in a variety of hues and tints. If you make a mistake, remove the oils with a mild turpentine solution. Once finished, the surface has to dry—usually for a day or two—as does any oil paint.

ALTERNATIVE PRODUCTS FOR THE UNITED KINGDOM

Some products mentioned in this book are unavailable in the United Kingdom*. Alternatives are listed below.

Product	US Brand Name	UK Brand Name
Berg Chemicals	Brilliant Blue Toner	Tetenal Blue Toner
		Fotospeed Blue Toner
	Copper Toner	Fotospeed Copper Toner
Edwal Chemicals	Hypo-Chek	Tetenal Fixing Bath Test
	Platinum II LPD	Agfa Neutol WA (No direct substitute is available in the UK)
Ilford Chemicals	ID-11 Plus	ID-11
Ilford Films	– –	XP-2
Kodak Chemicals	Farmer's Reducer	Any proprietary brand of Farmer's Reducer
	Polytoner	Limited supply available in the UK
Other Chemicals	Perma-Wash	Kodak Hypo-Clear
		Ilford Galeria Washaid

*Most products in this book can be obtained from Silverprint, 12B Valentine Place, London SE1 8QH. Zone VI products are available in the United Kingdom through mail order.

PART SEVEN
GALLERY

Black-and-white photography offers a wide range of expression. As you look at the photographs on the following pages, consider how each photographer used the medium to convey a particular state of mind and sense of place. Although printing technique is certainly important, it is simply a means to an end. The essential factor is the representation of a moment in time that is a manifestation of the thoughts and feelings of the photographer—a reflection of the world as seen and interpreted through an artist's eyes. As you appreciate these images, reflect on how you can bring this sense of seeing to your own work.

Cecilia's, Ouray, Colorado, 1987. © William Abranowicz.

Streetwise. © Mary Ellen Mark/Library.

Harlan Brandon. © 1990 Roy Volkmann.

Memorial to Times Past. © 1990 William Davis.

Naked Lunch—William Burroughs reading at St. Mark's Church. © Jeffrey Steinberg.

Home Sweet Home. © 1986 George Schaub.

Two Feet Plus One. © 1984 Joyce Tenneson.

Classic Torso with Hands, 1952. © 1952 Ruth Bernhard.

Tolaga Bay Jetty, New Zealand, 1986. © 1986 Vaughn Hutchins.

South Street Window. © 1975 David Wade.

At Ruben's Stand. © 1984 George Schaub.

Miss Liberty. © *1988 Jurgen Wassmuth.*

John F. X. Condon. © George Kalinsky.

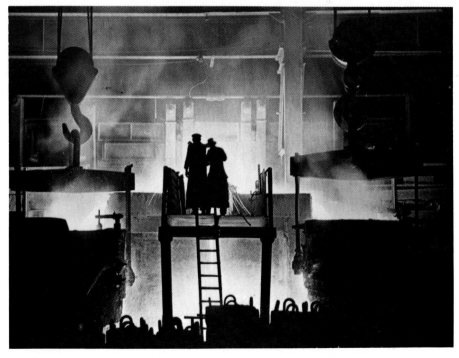

Stahlwerk. © Felix H. Man/Photokina Picture Exhibitions Cologne.

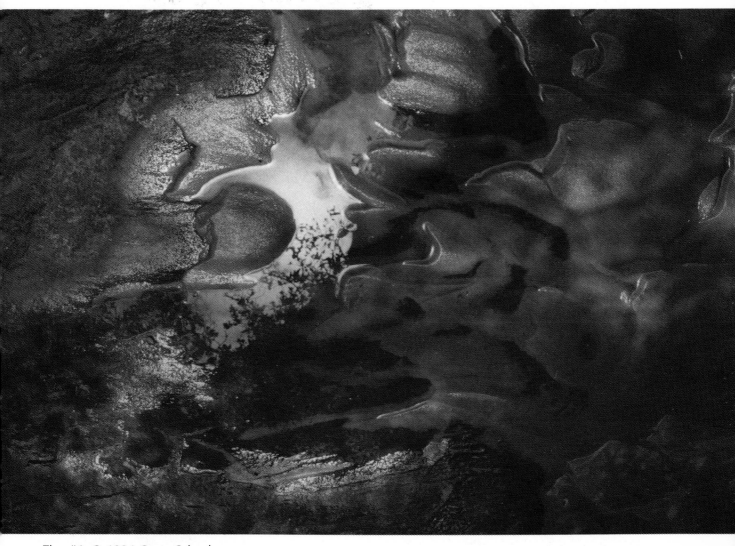

Zion #1. © 1984 Grace Schaub.

Zion Valley Wall.
© 1984 George Schaub.

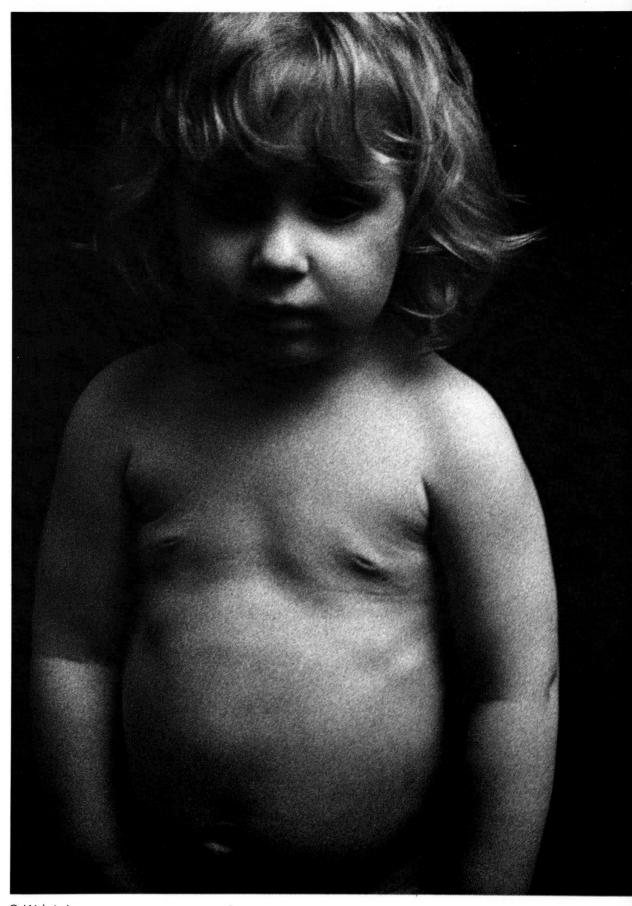

© Wah Lui.

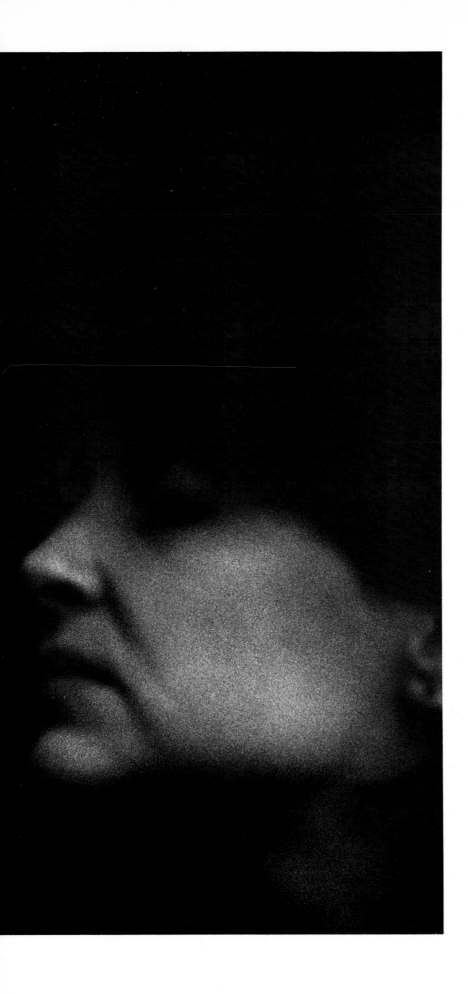

INDEX